KV-042-488

CONTENTS

ACKNOWLEDGMENTS

The suggestion that I should write a description of education in a special hospital was put to me by Professor J. E. Thomas and Dr. Barry Elsey of the Department of Adult Education, University of Nottingham. I am indebted to both for their continued support and advice.

As an employee of the Nottinghamshire County Council, Local Education Authority working in Rampton Hospital I am in the singular position of being responsible to two management authorities at the same time. Both 'County' and Hospital have been fully supportive and helpful in assisting me to complete this account. In particular I am most grateful to Derek Atha, Hospital Administrator, and Dr. John Comforth, Professional Assistant, Further Education Department for their understanding and help.

The necessary motivation to complete a study of this kind is often dependent on the attitudes of colleagues. I am fortunate that at all times teaching staff at Rampton have been concerned that I finish the task and given their full support. My special thanks to Mal Brady who provided the cover illustration.

Judith Spurr had the difficult task of typing up my hand written script into a readable form and I shall always be grateful to her for her perseverance and patience.

Finally to all patients and staff in Rampton Special Hospital I express my sincere appreciation for their contribution towards the rewarding professional life I have enjoyed over the past nineteen years.

EDUCATION IN A SPECIAL HOSPITAL

ISBN 1 85041 0259

Printed by Echo Press (1983) Ltd Loughborough.

INTRODUCTION

The purpose of this account is to describe the education service provided for patients in Rampton Special Hospital. A major part of this task is to indicate why education has become a substantial treatment provision and how it accommodates to the needs both of individual patients and the main requirements of the hospital.

Rampton is one of the four special hospitals in England and Wales. It is situated in a rural area of North East Nottinghamshire some six miles east of Retford and fifteen miles west of Lincoln. It began life in 1912 as a criminal lunatic asylum. In 1919 control of Rampton passed from the Home Office to the Board of Control. In its new role as a state institution for mental defectives with dangerous and violent propensities, it admitted only mentally handicapped patients convicted by the courts and those detained by the Mental Deficiency Act who could not be contained in 'local' mental hospitals. Ownership of the hospital was transferred in 1947 to the Minister of Health but continued to be managed by the Board of Control until 1959. In 1959 it became a special hospital under the provision of the Mental Health Act 1959. Since then it has been controlled by the appropriate national health body; currently this is the Department of Health and Social Security. In 1988 the duties of Health and Social Security were split up. Special Hospitals are now managed by the Department of Health.

The other English special hospitals are Broadmoor in Berkshire, and Moss Side and Park Lane, both of which are on adjacent sites at Maghull, nine miles north of Liverpool. Carstairs between Glasgow and Edinburgh is the special hospital for Scotland.

The Secretary of State controls all admissions to special hospitals. Until recently the policy was to send mentally handicapped and psychopathic patients of low intelligence to Rampton and Moss Side, and mentally ill and able psychopathic patients to Broadmoor and Park Lane. This arrangement is not so rigidly enforced as previously, as half the patient population at Rampton is now mentally ill.

Special hospitals serve no particular geographical area and admit patients from the whole of England and Wales. This arrangement is seen as particularly inhibiting in making and establishing close relationships with local authorities and with assisting patients in maintaining family ties and links. Proposals have been made to make special hospitals regional establishments. However their general geographical situation does not lend itself to a rational division of the country into regional areas.

Until 1981 all special hospitals were managed by D.H.S.S. officials from their headquarters in London. This contrasts markedly with the

1

arrangement for all other hospitals in the health service, who have local health authorities as their managers. In 1981, following the recommendations of the Boynton Committee (Boynton, 1980), Rampton Hospital was accorded by statute a local management body: the Rampton Hospital Review Board. The Review Board took on duties and responsibilities for the hospital similar to those carried out by local health authorities. In 1986 'Review' was dropped from the title, which became the Rampton Hospital Board. This attempt to provide Rampton Hospital with a more localised management dimension would seem to have worked satisfactorily, as have now been established boards at the other English special hospitals.

Though extensive legislation has firmly established the position of special hospitals in the health service of the country, the general public is still often confused regarding their nature and function. This is not surprising when the media, both press and television/radio, frequently misrepresent their status and function. Usually they are described by the hybrid term, hospital prison, or as prisons containing dangerous mental patients, or hospitals containing dangerous mental prisoners.

There is also a frequent misconception that, once admitted to a special hospital, a patient is likely to stay there for the rest of his life. If this were so, there would be far more than four special hospitals in England and Wales. Nevertheless, in general the length of stay for a patient is rarely less than four or five years.

Though the main aim of this account is to describe the patients' education service at Rampton Special Hospital, reference will be made occasionally to the education departments in the other special hospitals. Although serving a similar function these departments have developed along different lines, each having a unique identity. It should not be assumed therefore that what is described for Rampton is necessarily present in the educational arrangements for the other special hospitals. This situation however is not unusual in education in England. For example, to describe a single school as a representative of comprehensive education organisation would be totally unacceptable. Such an exercise would omit the rich diversity of philosophy which affects the organisation and administration of individual comprehensive schools.

The description of the education service in this working paper is presented in six parts. Chapter I describes the historical relationship between education and mental disorder over the past two hundred years from the time when visionary practitioners first realised the importance of education to the lives of mentally disordered patients.

It attempts to underline that education for the mentally disordered is not a recent innovation; that the past provides examples of established and valid educational work. Though high in quality, this work did not affect the treatment of the vast majority of mentally disordered persons hospitalised in large institutions. Reasons why there was no significant expansion of education until comparatively recently are put forward.

Chapter II examines the *context* in which education at Rampton Hospital is set. The status of special hospitals and what is officially required of them is provided. An outline of other disciplines employed in Rampton Hospital is given. Finally the position of the education department in the complex context of a special hospital is discussed.

In Chapter III an attempt is made to analyse the *task* of teachers. Additionally, areas which are related to the task are examined. These include therapy, meeting individual needs, security, inter-disciplinary cooperation and the nature of mental disorder.

The structure of the curriculum, which has developed in accommodating to the context in which education has to take place, and in meeting the requirements of the tasks the department has set itself, is described in Chapter IV. It is here that the detailed structure of the educational provision is presented. Also included is a description of teaching staff, their status and qualifications, their in-service training needs, the teaching methods they use and the resources at their disposal.

The evaluation of the educational service at Rampton Special Hospital is set out in Chapter V. An attempt to assess the quality and success of the education department is considered under three headings. First, as a measure of success, is an attempt to analyse the development of the department throughout its seventeen years existence. Attention is given to the response for increased resources necessitated by patient needs and treatment pressures. Additionally the evolvement of the current organisation of the curriculum is described. Second, statistics relating to progress in basic education over a number of years form the basis of an evaluation of the department's aim to develop social competence. Finally an attempt is made to evaluate the education department's success in its aim of enhancing the personal development of students.

The account of education in Rampton Special Hospital ends with comments on possible future development.

There is a possibility that this introduction to education in a special hospital will have a tendency to present a picture of a unique establishment with very little in common with practices in the overall field of teaching and learning. This would be unfortunate, for the real strength of education at Rampton Hospital is the emphasis placed on meeting the educational needs of students. In this respect the education department is at one with all schools and colleges in that the reason for their existence is the promotion of the same ideals.

Teachers at Rampton Hospital have to be competent in coping with problems and accepting constraints to their work which are very far from normal working conditions in other educational establishments. Nevertheless having come to terms with the differences of their student clientele and teaching in a closed institution, curriculum planning and development is based on principles which are universal to the total field of education. The work in the education department at Rampton Hospital can be said to have more in common with practices prevalent in schools and colleges than it has differences.

The description of education at Rampton Hospital should therefore have a wider range of appeal than at first glance seems possible. The educational models described in the promotion of social competence and personal development may prove instructive to those employed throughout many agencies who are involved in similar work. Currently such work is aimed at the under-achieving adult and adolescent. It is promoted by several agencies; among them A.L.B.S.U. (Adult Literacy and Basic Skills Unit), F.E.U. (Further Education Unit), the M.S.C. (Manpower Services Commission) as well as by individual schools and colleges.

More specifically this account provides further evidence for those working in the field of mental handicap who maintain that education for their charges is an ongoing process. Additionally the education work at Rampton Hospital has shown itself to be an activity which has accommodated itself to a total institution providing those detained with a wider choice of activity in their daily lives. This is of crucial importance in institutions where the organisation has the potential to severely restrict possibilities for personal freedom to the extent whereby inmates can suffer marked mental and physical deterioration. Finally education provides such a wealth of stimulating activity that it offers those recovering from mental illness opportunities to reconstruct their lives on lines which lead to stable and mature mental health. Overall, *Education in a Special Hospital* could be of interest to all involved in educational curriculum development and disciplines involved in the field of mental health.

Chapter I

A HISTORY OF EDUCATION IN INSTITUTIONS FOR THE MENTALLY DISORDERED

Visitors to special hospitals frequently express surprise that education is a firmly established activity in the daily life of patients. This reaction probably reflects a widely held view that the public regard hospitals as being the preserve of doctors, nurses and allied professions, and rarely consider education might have a part to play, particularly with the mentally disordered adult. Yet education for adults in institutions and hospitals for the mentally disordered is not a recent innovation. It has a history linked with the movement born towards the end of the eighteenth century which opposed the then common practices of manual and physical restraint of patients in "mad houses". The movement sought to replace such barbaric practices with activity and social intercourse.

Education, at the time, was considered by an eminent minority of practitioners in the field of mental disorder to be an important activity in the new approach to treatment. In the context of that time, characterized as it was by the massive social and political revolutions, they considered human irregularities as being due solely to human differences of education and experience (Itard, 1962: XIV). It was not surprising therefore that individual practitioners, professional and lay, should reach the conclusion that the behaviour of the mentally disordered could be modified through educational intervention.

The most significant early development in the introduction of a more humane approach to the mentally ill was made in York. Here, William Tuke, an eminent Quaker, founded 'The Retreat', an asylum for the mentally ill. Tuke, a non-medical man, aimed totally to use reason or distraction as his main aim of treatment (Masters, 1977: 74). Some thirty years later an official report *The Report of the Select Committee on the State of Pauper Lunatics from the Metropolitan Parishes 1827* recommended a role for education in the treatment of mental disorder (Jones, 1972: 106, 107). This significant document appears not to have influenced the majority of those who had responsibility for the care and welfare of the mentally disordered. The most notable exception to this general observation was Dr. John Connelly, physician at Hanwell Asylum. With the chaplain, the Reverend John May, he started classes in reading and writing for the illiterate, and drawing, singing and geography for the literate. Unfortunately, his visiting committee considered his efforts unnecessarily expensive, thus forcing Connelly to abandon his project (Jones, 1972: 120).

In general, little account was taken of the distinctions between the lunatic and the idiot at this time in providing a case for treatment, even though the distinctions were well known. It was observable that the Poor Law Institution, County and Private Asylums housed all categories of mental disorder plus the deaf, dumb, blind, epileptic and even the "severely physically handicapped". Other than basic care, the main task of the staff was to create order and stability. Only men of vision like Tuke and Connelly were likely to develop treatment procedures which would give patients a chance to improve general health and the maturity to live outside in the world. Conditions were such that new ideas on treatment had little chance of being generally accepted.

Foreign Influences

The experience of a French physician, J. M. G. Itard, in his attempt to civilize a sub-normal boy, described in his classic *The Wild Boy of Aveyron* (Itard, 1962), had a marked effect on the treatment of the mentally handicapped. Itard's ideas were developed in France by his pupil, Eduard Seguin. Seguin's ideas were influential, not only in his own country but also on the continent of Europe, and the U.S.A. His success in the education of mentally handicapped children through sense stimulation confirmed that education was their main requirement, and not medical management. He agreed that idiocy was an incurable disease, and while medicine should seek a cure, it was his duty in the meantime to see that the mentally handicapped should participate in the benefit of education (Crissey, 1975: 801).

In England, though Seguin's work was well received, it made as little impact on the general situation as that of Tuke and Connelly. Highgate Asylum was opened in 1855 to provide separate accommodation and education for mentally-handicapped children, based on Seguin's ideas (Pilkington, 1974: 22). However, even this modest venture

> "which started as an optimistic venture in education degenerated into custody, a mere shutting away".

> (King's Fund – Fact Sheet 3)

Impact of Education – Late Eighteenth and Early Nineteenth Centuries

In summary, the late eighteenth and the first half of the nineteenth century was an optimistic time for the mentally disordered. However, better care and treatment including education made no significant development. At Hanwell, cost was given as the reason, and this was often a sufficient reason in itself to debar progress. Additionally, there was powerful opposition by the medical profession to a more humane approach, of which it should be remembered education was only a part. For example, in the early 1840's, Sir Alexander Morrison called a policy of non-restraint a "gross and palpable absurdity, the wild scheme of a philanthropic vision, unscientific and impossible" (Masters, 1977: 153).

In particular it needed an exceptional head of an asylum to even contemplate the introduction of education when faced with the enormous organisational and administrative difficulties associated with overcrowding, unqualified staff and mixed diagnoses.

Factors Affecting Development – Late Nineteenth Century

By the mid-nineteenth century education for the adult mentally disordered had made no general impact in institutions. This resulted not from the lack of a sound theoretical basis as to its validity, but as noted above, to other factors. The climate for education in institutions for the mentally disordered was even more unfavourable throughout the remainder of the century, as Parliament concerned itself almost entirely with the legal aspects of mental disorder (Jones, 1972: 153).

Even more devastating to the cause of education, particularly for the mentally handicapped, was the work on eugenics, intelligence testing and family studies of the mentally handicapped which purported to show that mental deficiency was hereditary, responding neither to training or education (Jones, 1972: 188). This thinking affected life in institutions for the mentally handicapped until comparatively recently; inmates were considered incurable and consequently education and training a waste of money.

Education for ALL

The trend towards a more rewarding and positive life for those in mental institutions emerged in the years before the Second World War. However, there was no close co-ordination or co-operation between those proposing a policy of integration with, rather than rejection by,

7

society, for the mentally disordered. Consequently, no significant progress was made even though the authoritive *Report of the Mental Deficiency Committee* (Wood Committee, 1929) had strongly recommended that institutions caring for the mentally handicapped should prepare patients for life in the community through education and training.

As part of the planning in the reconstruction of Britain following the Second World War, the 1944 Education Act and subsequent legislation provided the opportunity for professional educators to become involved in the education of those locked away in closed institutions. R. A. Butler and his advisers in framing the 1944 Act fundamentally challenged the narrow conception of education which had dominated people's opinions for centuries. The new idea was to consider education as a continuous process conducted in three successive stages: primary, secondary and further. Post school education was seen as being essential to the development and growth of a democratic citizenship. One of the outstanding principles of the 1944 Act was therefore the recognition that education was a life long process (Lester Smith, 1962: 120).

Development of Professionally Directed Education in Mental Hospitals and Prisons

Local education authorities were empowered by the new legislation to provide education in areas where previously they had had no authority. This included work within institutions like prisons and mental hospitals which, being under the remit of government departments other than that of education, was an entirely new venture.

Although intervention by l.e.a.s in areas other than schools and colleges has been severely limited, mainly due to the inability of the state to finance adult education to any reasonable degree, the immediate post-war legislation has been important in providing a foundation for effective adult and further education in mental hospitals and prisons. Without a firm commitment from the state it is highly unlikely that professional educators would have been employed in institutions such as these. Although the Home Office, in conjunction with l.e.a.s, has developed a comprehensive adult education service throughout the prison and young offenders service, the Department of Health and Social Security or its predecessors have failed to provide a comparable service for its large mental hospitals. Many of these hospitals have been left to their own devices, and where education has been provided it has been dependent on amateur and semi-professional educational support.

Where adult and further education is obviously very relevant to the needs of patients, as in hospitals for the mentally handicapped, there has been a significant improvement in recent times. In 1978 a report to David Ennals, the Secretary of State for Social Service, by the National Development Group for the Mentally Handicapped stated that residents aged nineteen and over in hospitals for the mentally handicapped had some opportunity for education. In the worst areas 4.8% received education while in the best 23.3%. The level of provision would appear to depend on the relationship between the local further education colleges and hospitals (Mittler, 1978: 58).

For the mentally handicapped in hospitals there is now the possibility education is provided by professionally trained persons under the aegis of the local education authority. Nevertheless, the improvement is not such that it matches with the statement made by the Association of Professions for the Mentally Handicapped that

> "residents in hospitals for the mentally handicapped have the same rights to education as those in local authority or other residential provisions: the full range of community facilities should be available to them as it is to those mentally handicapped people who live outside the hospital".
>
> (A.P.M.H., 1974)

Educational Provision in Hospitals for the Mentally Ill

The statement by the A.P.M.H. applies equally to that other and perhaps major area of mental disorder, namely mental illness. Though they are detained in hospital, mentally ill patients should not be deprived of their right as citizens to the opportunity for further education. When the nature of mental illness is considered in relation to education, there does not appear to be a basis for accepting that education is an immediate and pressing need for patients. Consequently, although detained mentally ill patients should maintain the right to educational opportunity, there has been little if any progress in providing them with the same level of specialist help as is currently in existence in the field of mental handicap. Clyne (Clyne, 1972: 61) observes that the disparity between the provision for the mentally handicapped and mentally ill is based on the very obvious need for education in the "treatment" of the former, whereas with the latter education could be considered irrelevant.

Nevertheless, the work initiated by William Tuke at the Retreat in the 1790s in utilising education in the treatment of the mentally ill continues to be relevant at the present time. Not all persons suffering from mental illness have continuous severe symptoms. Periods of partial or complete remission from the effects of the disease are opportune times for education intervention. This fact has been recognised by a few psychiatric hospitals in the country who have arranged for classes to be organised by local further education colleges and the Workers Education Association (W.E.A.).

Development of Therapies based on Subject Areas Normally Considered Educational

Additionally, within hospitals for the mentally ill there has developed in recent years a system which has adopted as therapies subjects which are normally considered educational. The best known of these is art therapy, which is supported by professional training for its practitioners. Among others are drama, music, creative, literacy, horticultural and domestic therapies. These therapies are normally under the direction of occupational therapists or nurses. This is an interesting development which is discussed later in the section – education as therapy.

Perhaps because of the involvement with subjects as therapies, at least one occupational therapy department has moved in the opposite direction, i.e. from therapy to education rather than from education to therapy. In considering the rehabilitation of the chronically mentally ill Gan and Pullen (Gan and Pullen, 1984) observe that one of the three main areas requiring attention is the recreational and educational. They state there is little realisation that mentally ill patients need help in this area. One of their main aims at the activity centre for the mentally ill at Littlemore Hospital is:

> "To provide educational and recreational pursuits for a wide range of patients in order to enhance their quality of life".
>
> (Gan & Pullen, 1984: 216)

This laudable educational approach is organised without local education authority assistance. It is a situation which should not become permanent if other such centres are to adopt educational aims. Education is important to the mentally ill, thus there should be close co-operation between occupational therapists and educationists in its provision.

The Introduction of Professionally Directed Education into Special Hospitals

Broadmoor, Moss Side and Rampton provided education for patients before they became special hospitals in 1959. This provision continued in the years after the adoption of their new role. Teaching staff, however, were employed by the D.H.S.S. Staffing levels were small. For example at Rampton Hospital in 1968 a headteacher had responsibility for one full-time and two-part time staff.

In 1966 the Nottinghamshire local education authority became involved in the provision of education in Rampton Hospital. At the same time as the hospital continued with its own programme, the Retford Adult Education Centre organised twenty-eight classes staffed by sixteen part-time teachers. Two hundred and twenty patients attended in the year 1966/67. Although there was no significant increase in the number of classes, attendance at classes had doubled by 1969. This development was well received and was acknowledged in the 1968 Parliamentary Estimates Committee Report (P.P. Report, Appendix D: 285).

The introduction into Rampton Hospital by the l.e.a. of a wider and diverse range of educational opportunities and its success demonstrated there was a need to consider existing arrangements for education in the hospital. The hospital's response was to request the Nottinghamshire local education authority to accept responsibility for the total management organisation and development of education in the hospital. In September 1969 the l.e.a. commenced its new role with the appointment of two new full-time staff and a transfer of two of the hospital's teachers to the l.e.a. pay roll. Education in Rampton Hospital was therefore, from this date, firmly under professional control.

Moss Side was quick to follow Rampton's lead and a similar arrangement was made with the then Lancashire l.e.a. Park Lane recently asked the Sefton l.e.a. to accept responsibility for education for their patients.

Of the four English special hospitals, only Broadmoor continues with an education service which has no contractual links with its local county education authority.

Conclusion

Evidence from the past two hundred years clearly indicates that education has a part to play in the lives of the mentally disordered in hospitals. Since the end of the Second World War official educational policies have made it more likely, but not inevitable, that the adult mentally disordered in hospitals and institutions receive opportunities for education.

Chapter II
THE CONTEXT

Special hospitals are total institutions. They have a life of their own, which bears little resemblance to the reality of day to day living in the general community. Their separation from life as it is normally lived poses two major problems. First it is difficult to prepare patients for life in the outside community when the total structure of the hospital is alien to the process. MIND, the organisation promoting the welfare of the mentally disordered, goes further in stating that realistic treatment in special hospitals is impossible. It bases its opinion not only on the factor of achieving realistic treatment but on that of the second problem, the danger that patients will become institutionalised. While there are many working in special hospitals who are of the opinion that sensitive and efficient organisation can prevent institutionalisation, there is a powerful lobby, including MIND, who state this to be a completely unrealistic position. Though there is a reasoned case for closing down special hospitals, based on the difficulties of implementing realistic treatment in a total institution, the current position is that staff working in them have to recognise and be sensitive to seemingly almost intractable problems. Not withstanding the powerful constraints on their work, they have a duty to prepare patients for life in an open community in as effective a way as is possible.

Official Expectations of Special Hospitals

Broadmoor, Moss Side and Rampton Hospitals have a long history as institutions dealing with those identified as being a threat to society because of their unstable state of mind. However, it was not until the 1959 Mental Health Act that they were integrated into the national framework for the cure and treatment of mental disorder. At this time managerial responsibility was transferred from the Board of Control to the National Health Service. Mrs. Renee Short, Chairman (sic), of the House of Commons Estimates Committee, removed any ambiguity as to the status of special hospitals in stating,

> "We would like to emphasise that the special hospitals are part of the Hospital Service, not part of the penal system, though they are, so to speak, on the frontier of the two. Many of their patients are not offenders and we consider it extremely important that the special hospitals should not only regard themselves, but be regarded by other hospitals as part of the stream of modern psychiatry, using normal psychiatric techniques and dealing with particular challenging groups of patients".

(P.P. Report 1967/68: 204)

12

A review of Rampton Hospital took place in 1980 under the chairmanship of Sir John Boynton. This was initiated by the government in response to the Yorkshire Television film on Rampton which contained a large number of serious allegations of ill-treatment of patients by staff. The review team stated in their report (Boynton, 1980):

> "The present statutory basis for the provision of special hospitals does not say explicitly what the specific functions of special hospitals should be".
>
> (Boynton, 1980: 7)

Nevertheless the Boynton report stated that the statute makes it explicit that special hospitals have two main duties: to provide treatment and to do this in conditions of special security.

As it is the provision of the conditions of special security which so isolate special hospitals and cause them to be total institutions, the official expectations of staff to provide effective treatment are of a high order.

Conditions of Special Security

The Boynton Report described conditions of special security:

> "We take security in the context of a psychiatric hospital to mean arrangements designed to prevent compulsory detained patients (a) from leaving the hospital in which they are being treated except with the consent of and on such conditions as those responsible for their treatment may wish to lay down and (b) from causing harm to themselves, other patients or staff. 'Special security' we take to imply that in special hospitals it is intended that relatively more resources will be devoted to security than in other psychiatric hospitals."
>
> (Boynton, 1980: 7)

Showing agreement with Renee Short, the Hospital Advisory Report on Rampton Hospital (1971) and the Elliot Report on Rampton Hospital (1973), Boynton stressed that special security should not be regarded as a measure which by its nature converted special hospitals into penal establishments. The public must be protected from patients who have demonstrated propensity for criminal, dangerous or violent behaviour. Patients, because of their severe behavioural disorder, need protection from themselves and there is a need to protect staff by the implementation of efficient security procedures. Nevertheless patients are detained not as a punishment for what they have done; their loss of liberty is an urgent necessity in meeting their treatment needs.

13

Treatment

Rampton Hospital produced a document outlining its aims in 1972. Boynton stated "it was the nearest thing to an 'official' statement of the hospitals' policy towards treatment" (Boynton, 1980: 8). This document was revised in 1986. The basic principle of both the original and revised document is that the ultimate goal is to prepare a patient to a level where he can return to and survive in the community. The process preparation has been identified by several names over the past sixte years, rehabilitation, resocialisation, habilitation, socialisation ment and therapy. In the context of Rampton Hospital the revised statement of aims states that there is little benefit to be gained from an attempt to distinguish whether a process is treatment or therapy reaching the conclusion that anything which promotes the return of the patient to the community shall be considered treatment.

In a special hospital more than one discipline or profession is involved in the treatment process.

Disciplines in Rampton Hospital

Medical

Full clinical responsibility for patients is allocated to consultant psychiatrists. Their duties under the Mental Health Act 1983 are such they are designated responsible medical officers (R.M.O.s). Currently in post at Rampton there are ten R.M.O.s sharing a patient population of approximately 550 patients.

Holding ultimate responsibility for each of their patients' welfare, consultants are the most powerful and influential professional group in the hospital. Due consideration must be taken of their opinions in the implementation of any treatment procedure.

In recent years R.M.O.s have been increasingly involved in the establishment of a multidisciplinary approach to treatment. Currently their policy is to review regularly each of their patients at a clinical conference to which each of the disciplines involved in treatment procedures are invited. This is a crucial development, the effect of which, on the education department, will be discussed later.

Nursing

Nursing is by far the largest discipline in the hospital. Although all staff have a duty to the maintenance of effective security, nurses have traditionally accepted that they are the ultimate force in promoting and maintaining maximum security. Boynton (1980: 78, 79) expressed concern that there was evidence suggesting that the fine balance required in fulfilling both treatment and security was not being achieved. The report stated security issues were often used inappropriately to defer or negate action on the development of treatment procedures. Nevertheless experience of working in special hospitals confirms the relentless pressure on staff to maintain security. It is understandable therefore that such pressure does affect the discussions on treatments, which require changes in traditional security practices.

Nurses are responsible for thirty wards. The main wards are part of a large central block which is enclosed in the inner security wall. Between the inner and outer security walls are self-contained wards called villas. Patients move through the hospital following a pattern of admission ward, main ward, villa and finally a villa established outside the outer security wall. Rampton is therefore an extensive establishment dominated by long corridors, locked gates and, in the villa areas, gardens, lawn and extensive pathways. Though there are parts of Rampton which could not be considered beautiful, in general it has a pleasant aspect.

A main feature of security is that all movement of patients within the security walls takes place under escort. Except when patients are going to work, all escort duties are carried out by nursing staff. It is extremely rare therefore for a patient to be in a position where he is not being observed by a member of staff: on most occasions this will be a nurse.

Occupations

The occupations department is another large department consisting of over one hundred staff. It is staffed by occupations officers. Some are ex-nurses and others craftsmen. All have received or are in the process of receiving further in-service training through the City and Guilds 730 Teachers in Further Education Certificate and the 731/5 Trainers of the Mentally Disordered Certificate.

Patients attend workshops and work areas under the supervision of occupations staff on a daily basis Monday to Friday. There is a wide range of provision, from the traditional crafts of metalwork, woodwork, tailoring, printing to outdoor work in the maintenance of the large areas of sports fields and gardens both inside and outside the security wall. Additionally there are areas in which staff work with severe mental handicap students. The atmosphere of these areas and the work carried out has a great deal of similarity to Day Centres for the mentally handicapped in the community at large.

Psychology

Though there has been some improvement in meeting agreed staffing levels over the past few years, the department, because of marked staffing difficulties, has been severely restricted in its ability to tackle the wide range of treatment needs shown by patients. The department has remained small while the demands on its services have increased. There are certain treatments which demand the intervention of trained clinical psychologists. It is essential to the future development of Rampton that the psychology department is able to meet its critical staffing level.

Social Work

The social work department sees its role

> "as to facilitate, in cooperation with the patients, families, other hospital disciplines and community services, the effective rehabilitation of men and women detained in Rampton into normal community life."
> (Boynton, 1980: 104)

Boynton (1980: 105) identified three areas of responsibility of social workers. Firstly they are required to make contact with the families of patients as part of the initial assessment process. As Rampton, in line with the other special hospitals, has a catchment area which is national, social workers are frequently involved in very long journeys. Secondly there is a place for them in the extensive range of counselling of patients required in meeting treatment needs. Such work gives them a clear identification with work within Rampton Hospital. Thirdly they have the particularly crucial task of facilitating the discharge or transfer of patients from Rampton Hospital to their homes, hostels or lodgings or transfer to other hospitals. Conveying to the receiving authority that special hospital patients are now ready to function in the community with limited supervision invariably poses many problems for social workers.

Currently there are thirteen social workers in post. Additionally there are two community nurses in the nursing division who carry out pre-discharge duties similar to those of the social workers with certain patients transferred to local mental hospitals.

Education

Education, psychology and social work, are comparative newcomers to special hospitals. All have had problems of assimilation into institutions which have traditionally been organised and managed by medical, nursing and occupation disciplines. As well as being a newcomer to special hospitals, education at Rampton, Moss Side and Park Lane has a further distinguishing feature. Education staff, unlike those of the other major disciplines, are employed not by the hospital, but by the local education authority. The l.e.a. provides an educational service for the hospital. It recoups the major cost of this service from the Hospital but directly finances a number of part-time staff recruited for evening school classes.

Education Staffing

Currently there are 14 full-time teaching staff and 25 part-time teaching staff in post. They are supported by a clerk/typist' and an audio-visual technician both who work twenty hours a week. Teaching staff are employed under Burnham Further Education terms of service. Technically they are appointed as lecturers, but in the context of their work at Rampton 'teacher' is a much more accurate description in relation to their duties and is the term usually used in the education department and the hospital generally. The teaching team is led by a senior education officer (S.E.O.) holding a head of department II scale. He is supported by a deputy (D.S.E.O.) on a senior lecturer scale. Four lecturer II's are appointed, each one holding a post of responsibility as a section head for an area of the curriculum: the areas are (1) communication skills with the profoundly and severely mentally handicapped plus responsibility for the hard of hearing, (2) physical education and perceptuo-motor therapy, (3) basic education plus life and social skills, (4) counselling and sex education plus evening school supervision. The D.S.E.O. has responsibility for general academic and vocational education.

Education – Resources

Physical resources for the education department are the responsibility of the hospital. It provides an educational building consisting of seven general teaching areas, a domestic science room, three offices, a staff room and a small work-shop for the technician. Additionally the education department is responsible for a sports hall/gymnasium: a building large enough to hold two double and one single badminton courts. In the daily programme at least four full-time staff will be working in areas of the hospital controlled by other disciplines e.g. wards.

Equipment and materials are purchased directly by the hospital through its supplies section following appropriate requisitions from the education department.

Education – Links with Hospital Organisation

A feature of Rampton Hospital organisation since the early nineteen seventies has been the development of a multidisciplinary approach to management and the treatment processes. Although education is a service controlled and administered by the l.e.a. this has not been an obstacle in its integration into the multidisciplinary process.

The S.E.O. is a member of the Hospital Policy Committee (Policy). This committee consists of the heads of department of disciplines discussed above plus the Hospital Adminstrator, the chairman of the Consultants Advisory Committee, and chairmen of Divisional Management Teams. Three members of 'Policy' are senior to the rest on the basis that they form the Hospital Management Team (H.M.T.). They are the Medical Director, Chief Nursing Officer and Hospital Administrator. As a team, H.M.T. are charged with the responsibility for the day to day management of the hospital.

It is the task of 'Policy' to formulate the financial requirements of the hospital for the following financial year. Additionally, clearly defined objectives in the form of an operational plan must accompany the annual budgeting statement in its submission to the Department of Health and Social Security. In order that this requirement is fulfilled, all heads of departments including the S.E.O. submit annual operational plans and budgeting requirements to 'Policy'. The S.E.O. is therefore closely involved in perhaps the most crucial annual exercise, that of fixing a budget for the hospital based on a reasoned statement of policy.

'Policy''s other major role is to discuss, and advise H.M.T., on all issues which may affect the current management or future development of the Hospital's operational plan.

There have been several attempts, using various criteria, to divide a large hospital into more manageable units. Currently Rampton Hospital is divided into three divisional management teams: one for the mentally handicapped, another for mental illness, and one for resocialisation. The education department is represented on each of these divisional teams.

A division (D.M.T.) consists of a number of Unit Clinical Teams (U.C.T.). U.C.T.s are made up of two or three wards. There is a variation in the resocialisation division in that three treatment areas as well as wards are included in the composition of U.C.T.s. A teacher is allocated to each U.C.T. and represents the department at each of its meetings. U.C.T. meetings and the informal contacts they promote provide opportunity for staff of the hospital disciplines to liaise closely and plan treatment on interdisciplinary lines.

The outline of Rampton Hospital management structure given above indicates that teachers have a part to play at each level. There is another aspect of hospital organisation in which teachers are closely involved. This is the system of multidisciplinary case conferences. (This was mentioned above when discussing medical staff). Multidisciplinary case conferences have become increasingly crucial to a patient's treatment. The initial case conference collates and discusses the information on each patient presented by each discipline. A teacher presents a patient's education profile consisting of information on previous education, employment, mental state at time of assessments and interviews, current level of education, motivation, and educational interests. Additionally he outlines the patient's educational needs and proposes the means by which they can be met. Decisions are made at the end of the case conference which affect the patient's life and treatment for at least the next six months.

Follow up case conferences, ideally, occur every six months. Where a patient attends the education department, his teacher will be present at these conferences. The teacher gives a report both on educational progress and behaviour.

Within Rampton Hospital there is scope for a thousand case conferences in a year. Although not all students attend school, there is still a requirement for teachers to attend a large proportion of case conferences. The commitment to this particular feature of hospital organisation by teachers is consequently very high both in terms of attendance and the preparation of reports based on assessments and observation.

Over the years education staff have been increasingly involved in the overall work of Rampton Hospital. Additionally the work in the department has developed both in extent and scope of provision. As this account develops it will become clear that many factors have contributed to the development of the education department. Two of the factors are associated with the context in which education operates. The first of these is the education department's independent position through its formal attachment to the l.e.a.; the second is inhibiting and relates to the organisational requirement whereby patients are escorted to classes by nurses who then remain to observe and maintain discipline.

Education – Independence

Rampton Hospital's education department, before the l.e.a. accepted responsibility for it in 1969, was under the full control of the Department of Health and Social Security. Correspondence on patient placement and class and course organisation between nurse management and the head teacher indicates that the head's position at this time was subordinate.

In contrast to this position, Elliott (Elliott, 1973: 11) stated that the arrangements made in 1969 to transfer responsibility for education to the Nottinghamshire l.e.a. were a source of considerable strength. The education department was fortunate in being a separate entity, being financed through the l.e.a. and having its roots in the general further education system.

The strength of the independence of the education department derives from its professional base. The professionalism of the department, securely linked with the influence of the l.e.a., enables teaching staff to decide on curricular priorities. Although the other hospital disciplines have a decided influence on educational decisions they are not in a position to impose curricular policy on the education department. Attempts to undermine this basic strength of the education department occur from time to time. In 1973 the Hospital Committee decided there was a case for assessing the contribution of the education department to the hospital. A sub-committee was set up to carry this out. Having been informed of the decision, the then Director of Education for Nottinghamshire told the hospital that this assessment should stop forthwith. He pointed out that any assessment of the education department must be carried out by those qualified to do it, for example his inspectorate or H.M.I., and offered to carry out an inspection. The Hospital Management disbanded the sub-committee with an assurance to the Director that they were satisfied with the service provided by the l.e.a.

This anecdote indicates that the professional responsibility of teaching staff has been questioned by Hospital Management at certain times. It also shows that without the backing of the l.e.a., the teaching staff would be in a less able position to defend their professional independence. The l.e.a. organised department is well into its second decade in the Hospital and it is unlikely with the present style of hospital management that a similar situation to that in 1973 could reoccur. Nevertheless in an institution which is organised on a medical model with doctors and nurses fulfilling the dominant roles, there is an inevitable tension in providing an education service organised from a wholly different philosophical base. This tension should not be destructive. It has the potential for good in providing a stimulus for frank and open discussion on the best ways of meeting patients needs.

The independence of the education department has had a marked influence on a crucial factor in the development of the education department, namely staffing. It would have been difficult to recruit a high level and quality of staff if the education department had not been recognised as an integral unit of l.e.a. provision.

The fact that the education department at Rampton is l.e.a. controlled removes many inhibitions from prospective teaching candidates, for they may make their application in the knowledge that contractually they are not leaving the main stream of the education service; their conditions of service remain the same as Further Education lecturers in colleges in the community. This situation has a tendency to ensure that for any given post the applications are higher than they would have been without this security. Normally a higher level of applicants will in all probability include a larger number of well-qualified and committed staff.

It is perhaps a compliment to the teaching staff that their skill has been recognised by other disciplines. This recognition is validated by the fact that the last four full-time appointments up to 1987 were made as a result of requests from other disciplines to include teachers in the work they were doing.

In addition to the knowledge that they are l.e.a. staff, the link with the county education authority ensures teachers have available to them the full resources provided by the county. Advice and assistance is available from the advisory and inspectorate service. Information on short courses and other in-service ventures is posted regularly to the Rampton education department from the l.e.a. The availability of this backup gives staff an added sense of security in their professional

21

development. Without it there is a feeling that education in a special hospital would be so isolated its atrophy would be assured.

The involvement of staff in curriculum development has always been a feature at Rampton Hospital. A weekly hourly meeting forms the basis of this development. Mainly stemming from this venture has been the recognition of how inadequate staff are in the knowledge and skill required to deal with the very special needs of patients. This position has formed the basis for arguing the special needs of staff as well as patients. Part of the argument is that put forward by the Director of Education for Nottinghamshire l.e.a. in 1970 that the work was so demanding it was necessary for staff to have a break from it after three to four years. The other major factor in the case is that teaching staff require further specialised training. Placed side by side these two special needs have formed the basis of the head of the education department's contention that a generous policy of secondment should be a feature of employment at Rampton Hospital. In times of economic cut backs in education the case for this policy has not been easily accepted. Nevertheless in the years 1973 to 1986 eight members of staff have had a full year's secondment.

Two staff have completed M.Ed. degrees, one emphasising curriculum development and the other human values, four have done diplomas in special education, one a diploma in education of the severely and profoundly mental handicapped and another a diploma in Art Education/Therapy.

The independence of the education department has been most significant in protecting the right of teaching staff to decide on curriculum priorities, in attracting qualified staff and furthering their professional development and the needs of the department by a generous policy of full-time secondment.

Education – Nurse Staffing

Ideally teaching staff prefer a situation where they are in complete control of the management and organisation of their teaching area. In Rampton Hospital this position has not been fully attainable and there has been an on-going struggle by the education department to maintain full control and management of teaching areas.

The problem is related to nurse staffing of the education department. Since the l.e.a. department was opened in 1969, Hospital Management have insisted on a nurse presence in the department. Nurses escort patients to and from the department and stay in the department during classes. A nurse manager is attached permanently to the education department to manage nurse procedures.

During the times patients are in the department, nurses are present to promote their welfare, to provide security and to assist teachers with their work. The task of assisting teachers with their work demands that nurses are fully aware of methods and objectives. Unfortunately nurse staffing has been on a day to day basis for many years, and this lack of permanency has made the task of the establishment of stable teacher-nurse partnerships impossible to achieve.

Nurses have been, therefore, inclined to believe that they are mainly in the education department to provide security. Part of this duty is to secure the safety of the teaching staff. In facilitating this duty, except for a brief period in 1986, nurses have been actually present in the teaching areas at all times.

The situation whereby another profession is present in the teaching area for purposes other than education is a threat to the teacher's confidence and feeling of ease in the teaching situation. It can also undermine her ability to manage and organise the classroom to standards which she finds acceptable.

Currently a new attempt is being made to solve the problem of providing security in the education department without seriously affecting individual teachers' right and duty to teach in an environment which facilitates learning objectives. It is proposed that a core of nursing staff be attached permanently to the education department. Their duties will include a firm commitment to work with teachers in achieving the department's aims and objectives. It is hoped a close partnership will evolve which will strengthen and enhance the service to students.

The reliance on nursing staff for the maintenance of procedures directly related to the hospital's function as a maximum security hospital has had a further adverse effect on the education department. Students are only able to attend classes if they are brought there by nurses. Punctuality therefore is dependant on the nurses. The Boynton Report (Boynton, 1980: 97, 98) stated that all this good work by teachers was being frustrated by a serious organisational problem, that of a lack of punctuality.

> "Because of nurses' ward duties, and delays in the afternoon caused by the meal rotas we found that patients regularly arrived up to 30 minutes late and not uncommonly 45 minutes to an hour late. This can occur at the beginning of any of the three sessions, morning, afternoon or evening. For similar reasons, patients are also often taken away early

from classes. This unfortunately results in a serious waste of resources since teachers are being paid for the time that is lost. It causes frustration to the teaching staff as well as impairing the efficiency of the education programme."

(Boynton, 1980: 97, 98)

Nurse management have responded firmly to the situation described by Boynton. There are now only minor problems associated with punctuality for the morning and evening sessions. Nevertheless the afternoon session still has its problems with students frequently attending late. The reasons are many but revolve round the fact that an escort staff may not leave his ward to collect students for classes until his relief turns up. His primary duty at the time is to security on his ward. The relief may be delayed for a number of very sound reasons which are not apparent to management at the time of planning of the education department escort procedure.

Punctuality is, therefore, one of the factors that the education department is almost powerless to affect. Nevertheless, as Boynton indicates, it has a marked influence on the effectiveness of the curriculum. It can be seen that the problem arises from the organisational structure developed to maintain a high level of security.

Providing an educational service in the context of maximum security results in major difficulties for the management and organisation of the education department. There are further constraints associated with security which will be described in the next chapter.

Summary

Special hospitals are total institutions providing maximum security. Because of their organisational structure, a powerful lobby in the field of mental health believes they are unable to carry out satisfactory treatment. Nevertheless the official line is that special hospitals are hospitals, providing treatment under conditions of special security, and not penal establishments. Treatment is defined as a process which ultimately seeks to place patients back in society at a level of personal adjustment which ensures their ability to cope in day to day social situations without stress to themselves or harm to others. Special security is a necessary expediency protecting the public, the patient and staff. Several disciplines are involved in treatment: responsible medical officers who are appointed as consultant psychiatrists, a high complement of nursing staff, occupation officers, social workers, psychologists and teachers. Teaching staff are relatively new to special hospitals.

Nevertheless in Rampton Hospital they have developed a soundly organised and well resourced department, both in level of staff and equipment and materials. Teachers are involved in all but the top-most levels of the hospital's management structure. Additionally they play a major role in the multidisciplinary clinical case conference organisation. The context in which teachers work is considerably strengthened by their independence as employees of the Nottinghamshire local education authority. However, counteracting this advantage are the problems associated with security and the escorting of patients.

Chapter III

THE TASK

The task of education departments in special hospitals is complex. There are many factors acting on the development of educational policies which reflect the needs of patients and the attainment of stated hospital aims. Teachers in education departments must be quite clear as to their roles and be certain in the knowledge that their work is crucial to the function of the hospital. The task of education departments must, therefore, have recognition; it must be clearly stated, and based on the needs of patients. Additionally other factors which contribute to or inhibit the task must be recognised and understood.

Recognition of Education's Position

There have been several notable official reports commenting on education in Rampton Hospital. The first was the House of Commons Estimates Committee Reports (P.P. Report 1967/68), followed by the Hospital Advisory Report 1971 (H.A.S., 1971), the Elliott Report *A Survey of Rampton Hospital* (Elliott, 1973), and the Boynton Report *Report of the Review of Rampton Hospital* (Boynton, 1980). Without exception these reports expressed views which supported the work of the education department and its contribution to the hospital's treatment plans. In general, comments were in line with the philosophy outlined in the history of education in Chapter I, that education had a significant part to play in the lives and treatment of patients in hospitals for the mentally disordered. A comment from the H.A.S. report is representative of those quoted in other official documents.

> "Education, entering later into the treatment plan within security hospitals, has an advantage in that it is not bedevilled by historical problems of development as are other disciplines. As a social service it has passed through its ambiguous stages of 'negative benevolence' to become established as a right to the individual to be given the maximum opportunities to develop his potential. All this encourages the freshness and creativity with which the teachers here perform their tasks. This could be an asset to the hospital as a therapeutic institution if not regarded as an encroachment and a threat to other disciplines."
> (H.A.S., 1971: 71)

The supportive references provided by the above reports have been more sustaining of morale in the education department at Rampton

26

than their originators would have believed possible. For as the H.A.S. quotation inferred there have been and still are times when the validity of education in the hospital is challenged. At such times teachers are able to reassure themselves as to the value of their work through the daily contacts they have with their students. This contact and the teacher/student relationships that develop from it sustain staff in the belief that what they are undertaking is crucial to the personal needs of each student. Teachers are not unaffected by criticism but they have the strength to continue with their daily duties in a manner befitting their status as professionals. Elliott, in his report, recognised this strength:

> "psychology and education have a life of their own. They are strong enough to develop their own professional ethic. They command a considerable body of specialised knowledge. For them, the absence of a common therapeutic strategy certainly reduces the usefulness of their contribution, but they are intellectually strong enough, independent enough, and have good enough leadership, to set their own objectives and to work to them".
>
> (Elliott, 1973: 10)

Official recognition of their role in special hospitals and their own professionalism have been major factors in sustaining and confirming teachers' commitment in Rampton Hospital. Nevertheless although it must be acknowledged as inevitable in a closed institution that education provided by the l.e.a. will be questioned frequently as to its validity for patients, there have been important developments arising within the hospital which have recognised the contribution trained teachers can make to treatment programmes. These developments have in general stemmed from the 'grass roots' and have begged questions as to the best methods of meeting the needs of patients.

The recognition by other disciplines that education had something worthwhile to offer was and continues to be reassuring. In the early days of the department when attempts were being made to identify its role, it was ward nursing staff who highlighted the high level of social incompetence which existed in the majority of patients. Nurses pointed out the consequences of returning patients to the community without adequate personal knowledge and skills. It was their opinion that educational resources should be used to remediate basic educational deficiencies, and not be frittered away on academic studies. The report *Survey of Incapacity Associated with Mental Handicap at Rampton and Moss Side Special Hospitals* (Parker, 1974) did no more than confirm what had been widely known, that forty-eight per cent of the Rampton

27

Hospital population were partially or severely handicapped by their lack of literacy skills. Faced with the evidence that a large number of patients were in need of basic education, it is not surprising that the development of the education department at Rampton Hospital has been dominated by the need to cope with this problem.

Another major development in educational provision in the education department resulted once more from the strong convictions of ward nursing staff.

In 1969 Concord Ward housed a number of highly disturbed severely mentally handicapped patients. These patients could not be accommodated in any of the occupational areas. Their potential was too low and their behaviour too disturbed for them to benefit from education based on the acquisition of literacy and numeracy.

A programme of perceptuo-motor activities was organised, which is described more fully in the next chapter. The fuller description of the work indicates that considerable development took place for the severely mentally handicapped patients who had previously nowhere to go during the day. Later similar facilities for chronically mentally ill patients, who were difficult to place in traditional work, training and education areas, were provided. The development is not only significant in that the education department responded to a need identified by hospital ward staff but current provisions for the groups concerned is a joint venture of nurses and teachers.

From the early days when just six severely mentally handicapped patients attended the gymnasium for perceptuo-motor activities for a half-morning there has been a wide expansion of services. Teachers working with their nursing colleagues are involved in music, drama, craft, communication, art, music and movement, perceptuo-motor activities, games and swimming. This development has been a 'grass roots' one and although now officially part of the hospital's therapeutic service it is debateable whether it would have occurred without the initial contact between ward staff and teacher. The other special hospitals have not developed a system in which teachers and nurses work together as in the provisions at Rampton Hospital for severely mentally handicapped and chronically mentally ill patients.

Being accepted as a specialist by members of another profession, as teachers are at Rampton Hospital in the joint nurse/teaching ventures, is important. It gives counter weight to unfounded statements that teachers are taking jobs from other disciplines, concerning themselves only with those of high ability, depriving children of staff, adequate educational resources and even disturbing the ecological balance by its threat to trees through over use of paper.

In discussing the context of education in the previous chapter there is a further clear acknowledgement through teaching staff's involvement in the hospital's clinical and management structures that the department's contribution is integral to treatment procedures and policies.

The Task Defined

The recently revised document on the aims of Rampton Hospital (1986) requires the Hospital to effectively combine the functions of:
(a) *custody,* by preventing individuals from engaging in acts which could be harmful to themselves or others.
(b) *protection* by safeguarding the rights of detained patients.
(c) *treatment* by preparing them for return to less secure conditions in the outside community as soon as possible.

In following the requirements of this document the education department has identified two main tasks. The preparation of a patient for life in the community through a planned treatment programme begs the question as to the nature of such a preparation. The education department has taken preparation to mean a development (or redevelopment in some cases of mental illness) of social competence. The first main task of the education department, therefore, is to organise its work in a way which assists each of its students to reach a higher level of social competence. The second task is to promote through its activities opportunities for personal development. This is very much interrelated with the development of social competence. Nevertheless the emphasis in personal development is placed to offset those factors which, if not checked, result in individuals becoming institutionalised. In promoting personal development, educational activities may be used which are seen to be outside the parameters of the concept of social competence.

(a) *The Task Defined – the Development of Social Competence*

A succinct definition of social competence is provided by Kellmer Pringle (1965).

> "Social Competence is manifested by the extent to which an individual is willing to conform to the customs, habits and standards of behaviour prevailing in society in which he lives; by the degree to which he is able to do so independently of direction and guidance; and by the extent to which he participates constructively in the affairs and conduct of his community".
> (Kellmer Pringle, 1965)

29

It is observable that this level of social competence is not easily reached or maintained by the majority of the population, least of all by those who are mentally disordered in some way. However, most people manage to survive in society with lower levels of social competence and it is in recognition of this fact that special hospitals assist patients to acquire those skills which will enable them to cope with life outside to a degree which reduces personal stress and over-dependence on others.

There is a clear relationship between the hospital treatment aim of preparing patients for life in the community and the development of social competence. It could be accepted that the relationship is so close there is no distinguishing feature between the two. For preparation involves a process in which the patient comes to accept the need to conform to social customs, habits and standards; that treatment staff recognise the need to assist patients to acquire life and social skills in order that they become increasingly independent of direction and guidance. If such preparation is successful Rampton Hospital has played its part well. It can be satisfied that the third aspect of social competence, that of participating constructively in the affairs and conduct of the community, is a concept which although important and having the potential for fuller personal development, is not crucial to living a law-abiding and contented life.

Social Competence and the Mentally Handicapped

The mentally handicapped adult in special hospitals is particularly vulnerable to the stress of living in the community because of his negligible level of social competence. It is therefore imperative that the main thrust of treatment should involve strategies to relieve this acute picture of under-development. Independence of direction and guidance is a goal which needs to be strived for persistently and with consistency.

Education which is clearly defined in its aims and objectives is crucial to the process of habilitation of the mentally handicapped. Without education a mentally handicapped person cannot develop social competence, therefore limiting his ability to survive anywhere other than in an institution. There is the added disadvantage that in Rampton Hospital, completely isolated as it is from the real world, a lack of opportunity to use previously learned skills will lead to their loss. If opportunity for education is therefore denied the mentally handicapped person in a special hospital, there is a possibility that he will be less socially competent on leaving the hospital than when he was admitted. Such a position would be a clear case of failure, as the patient would be in a worse position to cope than when he was admitted. The stress associated with such failure could be so personally traumatic as to trigger off a pattern of reoffending.

Recent thinking on the function of hospitals for the mental handicapped has come to the conclusion that they are educational establishments in the broadest sense of the term (Mittler, 1978: 7 Para 2.3.1.). Their main function is to train patients to be independent by maximising individual potential. This means developing skills of social competence in relation to shelter, food, warmth, personal hygiene, dress, conduct, employment, leisure, and communication. H. C. Gunzburg (1968) describes his structure for developing social competence in mental handicap as a first-aid to living. The skills acquired are sufficient to develop a general level of independence plus some awareness of the need to consult support services when the individual is failing to cope.

The recognition that education is the main priority in mental handicap hospitals has caused some concern, largely because of the monumental size of the task and the lack of resources available. Mittler (1978: 37 Para 5.2.1.), O'Hara (1968) and Gunzburg (Clarke & Clarke, 1974: 646) have all made the point that the problem can only be overcome if the few teachers available work in close co-operation and with the assistance of other staff, particularly nursing.

The case for education for the mentally handicapped in hospitals is substantial. In special hospitals the need is even more evident, albeit more difficult to meet because of the almost total isolation of patients from society. The extent of the need to provide education for the mentally handicapped at Rampton can be judged from the description in the following chapter with its emphasis on those areas of basic education fundamental to the development of social competence.

Social Competence – the Mentally Ill

It is now accepted that mentally handicapped persons, because of their lack of development in mental processes, require more and not less education over a long period of time if they are to overcome their disability in part or full. This position acknowledges that an educational model is the most appropriate to their needs. In Rampton Hospital however, the recent trend is to admit increasing numbers of mentally ill patients, e.g. percentage admission of mentally ill in 1971 were male 27%, female 26%, as against 1981 figures of 62% male and 40% female. The increase is even more significant when taken in the context that the hospital population dropped from over 1,000 to 600 patients between these years. Though Broadmoor Hospital has always admitted a high percentage of mentally ill patients, the change for Rampton Hospital, as a former state institution for mental defectives, has had major implications with regard to treatment. The education department has been involved in a re-appraisal of its role, for while education for the mentally handicapped is essential, for the mentally ill the need has not been so readily acknowledged.

The re-appraisal of role has, however, not resulted so far in a major restructure of the basic education programme which forms the major part of the department's curriculum. This stems from the fact that the structure of the department is decided through the process of meeting individual needs and not according to the apparent general require-ments of generic groups such as mental handicap, mental illness or psychopathy. The process of assessing individual needs firmly indicates that a large proportion of the mentally ill have marked deficiencies in basic educational areas and associated skills in social competence.

In November 1984, the percentage of mentally ill patients on basic education were:

Level I (remedial) 37%   Level II (remedial) 55%   Level III (basic studies) 46%

These figures give some indication of the degree to which mentally ill patients admitted to Rampton Hospital require assistance with basic educational skills.

There are two possible reasons why mentally ill patients should display marked educational under-functioning. Firstly, they may be mentally handicapped in addition to their psychosis and/or they were educationally backward before the onset of their illness. Secondly, the profile of poor educational attainment could be the result of their illness; trauma to the areas of the brain controlling memory and perception being so intensive that previously acquired skills and knowledge are lost. Such damage may be reversible or permanent. Experience at Rampton Hospital indicates that there is a case for education in the treatment of the mentally ill based on the same criteria as those for the mentally handicapped. The main justification is that a significant number of patients present a picture of gross social inadequacy.

This is not to say that the distinctions of classification should be completely ignored. Initially, for instance, it should be evident that the more florid of psychotic symptoms must have responded to medical treatment before basic education can be contemplated for a mentally ill patient. Further, teaching staff should be aware that in some cases they will be attempting to rehabilitate a patient, i.e. assisting in the remission of symptoms leading to complete recovery and a 'normal' life. With other patients the remission may be small and the teacher is, as with the mentally-handicapped, involved in a process of developing, in contrast to re-developing, skills. In this task she is faced with the additional problems posed by the still extant symptoms of the psychosis.

There is much yet to be learned regarding the organisation and application of education to the mentally ill. Nevertheless, experience in special hospitals indicates that many mentally ill patients benefit from attending education sessions which stress the development of social competence.

Social Competence – Psychopathic Disorder

Over the years special hospitals have had responsibility for another category of mental disorder, namely that of psychopathic disorder. Although psychopathy is seen as a disorder affecting the emotional development of individuals, many patients in the special hospitals, particularly Moss Side, Rampton and Carstairs, have also demonstrated that they are markedly deficient in basic communication skills. Individualised assessments at Rampton Hospital have shown that a significant percentage of psychopathic patients have the same problem as those with other mental disorder classifications in the areas of social competence, particularly in regard to basic communication.

Psychopathy is considered to be untreatable (Cleckley, H., 1982). Nevertheless experience in special hospital education departments has shown that patients categorised as psychopathic have made considerable gains not only in relation to the primary educational aim of improving competence but also in improved social attitudes. Such experience should indicate to educators who may be faced with providing education for those diagnosed as psychopathic that "untreatable" should not be a signal for inaction. There may be at the least two reasons why psychopaths have shown positive social development. Firstly, there has been an error in diagnosis. Secondly "untreatable" should be accepted as meaning there are no universally acceptable specific lines of treatment for psychopaths, BUT the possibility of social improvement cannot be ruled out as chance circumstances may provide the necessary catalyst for change. The exceptionally close social interaction between student and teacher necessary in facilitating the development of basic educational/communication skills may prove fertile ground thus bringing about positive changes in social attitudes.

Social Competence – the Case for Education

There is a strong case for education in special hospitals, therefore, because of the valuable contribution it makes in the process of preparing patients for return to the community. This is mainly attributable to the emphasis placed on developing or redeveloping important areas of social competence for a large number of patients of all categories of mental disorder.

(b) *The Task Defined – Personal Development/Countering the Effects of the Institution*

Education is much more than a tool for helping people develop social competence skills. Sir John Adams stressed its overwhelming importance by going so far as to describe it as the dynamic side of philosophy (Ross, 1943: 16)

It is a fundamental of civilised living for,

> "Education in its unrestricted sense, means the process by which people are brought to an understanding and appreciation of what is valuable in human life".
>
> (Forster, 1981: 35)

In this sense it has a crucial part to play in the personal development of patients in special hospitals. It becomes even more important when it is considered that closed institutions like Rampton are structures having a tendency to inhibit rather than promote personal development. Education can play a significant part in reducing the effects of this detrimental process of institutionalisation.

In the special hospitals, education has therefore a wider function than the development of basic education in relation to social competence.

The Boynton Report, while fully recognising the education department's development in the area of basic education/life and social skills, recognised the need to further widen the scope in other aspects of education.

> "In particular we would like to see the further (i.e. adult) education programme widened and developed. For patients who are long-stay residents in hospital, recreational activities are much more significant, even crucial than for the normal clients of further education provision".

"Comprehensive programme cannot only help individuals in their development and rehabilitation; it can also make the day-to-day management of patients much easier for staff on duty".

"We think that the day-time courses could be further developed with courses for example in social and environmental studies, language literature and art and craft. This would help meet the needs of the more able patients for whom provision is at present limited."

(Boynton, 1980: 98-99)

These are important statements. They recognise that whereas adult education generally is highly desirable, its provision in closed institutions is crucial. Patients require a higher, not a lower level of provision, than exists in the community. The statements give reasons for this, one of which is the potential provided by education for individual development.

From another source, that of the Report on the State Hospital, Carstairs, (Scottish Home & Health Department, 1977) there is further strong support for education in special hospitals. The report, set up to examine the escape of two patients and the subsequent tragic murder of three persons, including a nurse, had this to say about the Prison Officers' Association's reaction in banning education in the Hospital:

"We consider that it was a retrograde step to deny educational facilities to patients who have the capacity to use them and whose lives are already restricted by detention in the State Hospital".

(Scottish Home & Health Department, 1977: 31)

This comment supports the view of the Boynton Committee expressed above that educational provision on a wide scale can help to reduce the effects of living in the narrow confines of an institution.

Part of the task of education in special hospitals can be considered, therefore, in the wider context of the provision of educational opportunity for all, from infancy to old age. It is evident that patients are denied normal rights and opportunities by the very nature of their commital to special hospitals. Nevertheless, there is no logical or economic reason why they should be denied educational opportunity. More positively, education can be seen as an effective antidote to the depersonalising effects of a closed institution. At the least this means limiting or retarding the process of institutionalisation whilst most favourably the trend has been to see patients make remarkable personal development.

There would appear to be few examples of empirical research which would give substantive support to the claims that education furthers personal development and acts as a counter agent to the effects of closed institutions. However, the comments made above from the reports on special hospitals are really part of a widely held philosophical belief that education is a process which, as it develops within or affects an individual, produces changes for the good. W. Forster (Forster, 1981: 84) writing of education in prisons puts the point more cogently:

> "The strong case for education lies in its real power to act as an agent of change not as a blind panacea for both crime and punishment. And as such a force, it should play its full part in our personal and national life".

Special hospitals are not prisons, nevertheless there is enough similarity in length of time served by inmates, and nature of the institution, for Forster's observations to apply equally to special hospitals.

The dehumanising effects of closed institutions and the problems associated with long periods of separation from society have been dealt with by several researchers (Goffman, 1961; Morris, 1969). It is not possible in this short account to deal with the possibilities of using education as an antidote for the full range of depressing effects. There is, however, in both special hospitals and prisons, one problem, that of time, which can be used as an example to illustrate how education may assist in diminishing the worst effects of incarceration, and more positively actually achieve a level of personal development. The problem of time to many patients in special hospitals may be even more acute than it is for prisoners. Unlike prisoners, patients have no fixed sentence, and therefore, their release date is not known. There are some patients for whom time is no problem: the elderly institutionalised who find the hospitals a true asylum and have no wish to leave, the chronically mentally ill whose mental lives bear little resemblance to normality. However, it is observed that the idea of leaving the hospital is a continual pre-occupation with the majority of patients. Consequently, the sociological study of Cohen and Taylor (Cohen & Taylor, 1981) at Durham Jail, which deals with the problem of time, has implications for patients in special hospitals.

These researchers note:

"The marking and the passing of time are then major elements in long term prisoners lives. Time presents itself as a problem. It is no longer a resource to be used but rather an object to be contemplated – an undifferentiated landscape which has to be marked out and traversed. Conventional markers cannot be used and neither can one's journey be expedited by recourse to traditional methods. Nevertheless the length of the journey continually pre-occupies the mind for only after it has been made can life be effectively resumed".

(Cohen & Taylor, 1981: 114)

Education has the resources to offer a large range of activities and knowledge to meet the needs of all levels of ability. The potential for helping inmates of closed institutions to fill their time with positive activity is therefore very great. Academic education, for example, can provide markers as progress is made at different examination levels from Royal Society of Arts examination to Open University. Craft education also offers the opportunity to chart the passage of time as the creation of objects depends on processes each having their own unit of time for completion.

Without activity time becomes a medium for moral, spiritual, mental and physical deterioration. Given the circumstances it is essential that patients and prisoners are given the opportunity to take part in educational activities.

Coping with the problem of time by involvement in education may be associated with another phenomenon common to closed institutions. Attendance at classes may be an observable indication that education is being used by the patient to escape from the close control which is a feature of closed institutions.

Attendance may be a reflection of their attempt to cope with a life in detention, rather than a basic need which they would seek to fulfil if they were living on the outside. Goffman (Goffman, 1961: 67, 68) has observed that inmates of American closed or total institutions will try to make life as bearable as possible by attempting to escape from the ever present close control of the system, by joining in games, orchestra or band playing, choral singing, lectures or art classes. This attempt to loosen the grasp of the institution is so well established, argues Goffman, that he names it the 'removal system'.

The provision of a wide range of classes by the education department is important because the involvement and social intercourse which takes place helps to counteract the effects of the artificial environment of a

37

special hospital. In meeting patients' individual needs it is therefore incumbent on educational planners not only to consider skills and knowledge required for life outside the hospital but also activities which help to make life more tolerable within the walls of the institution.

There is an authoritative consensus that education in closed institutions should be available for all and not be restricted in its activity to basic education. This is based on the assumption that activity counteracts the lethargy which is a pervasive feature of closed institutions. More positively educationally directed activity has the potential for individual development. Educators in special hospitals have therefore a clear task to provide an educational programme which takes account of these factors.

Task Related Areas (a) Therapy

The difficulty in distinguishing what is treatment, or therapy, or rehabilitation has been acknowledged above with an agreement at Rampton Hospital that all strategies utilised in preparing patients for the community are treatment. It has been proposed that the education department's involvement in the areas of social competence and personal or individual development is a major contribution to the treatment process. The work can be seen both as education and treatment.

The education department at Rampton Hospital is involved in areas of work whereby the activity is seen to add to treatment but cannot always be seen as belonging within the normal parameters of education. In this sense it is not the identification of the subject matter which poses problems but essentially the objective of its application. The objective is not seen as being strictly educational. Although the use of the term therapy has been discounted above, it is a useful term to use in illustrating the difference between the work of the education department in which education objectives facilitate treatment and other objectives which also promote treatment. These other objectives in this context are seen to be therapy or therapeutic.

The fields of therapeutic activity at Rampton Hospital in which teaching staff have become involved are art, music and drama therapy, counselling and remedial gymnastics.

Art Therapy

The department has attempted to meet the needs of the hospital in this area. A member of staff and specialist in art and art therapy provides individual sessions on two wards with highly disturbed female patients and group sessions with psychotic patients displaying difficulties in communication using conventional methods.

Music and Drama Therapy

The department has had a small but significant contribution in this area. Teaching and nursing staff have organised day-training seminars for staff from other hospitals.

Counselling

Trained staff from all disciplines in the hospital are involved in this work. Teachers are amongst these staff, having received their training on multidisciplinary courses.

Remedial Gymnastics

Work in this area is now done by the physiotherapist. Prior to her appointment two staff having dual teacher/remedial gymnastic qualifications assisted with the rehabilitation of physical injuries.

The task of teaching staff at Rampton Hospital has been widened to include involvement in therapy largely because specialist trained staff have been unavailable. It is a high reflection on the calibre of staff that they have carried out this additional work with skill and imagination.

Task Related Areas (b) Meeting Individual Needs

The education department at Rampton Hospital has long since recognised that task fulfilment is most efficient when due recognition is taken of the needs of individual patients. Whether the main task is to develop social competence or to enhance personal development, educational objectives must be based on a sound knowledge of what is required to bring each student to a higher level of function. There is, therefore, a clear mandate on the department to develop a structured process which will provide information on the needs of students in as comprehensive a manner as is possible.

An efficient curriculum can only be planned if it is structured to meet the needs of students. The first task therefore is to identify needs. At Rampton Hospital the process of identification is extensive and is seen as an essential prerequisite to the placement of students on classes.

One would anticipate that prolonged contact between a teacher and student in the classroom would ultimately result in the teacher becoming aware of the student's needs. However the development would be slow and consequently inefficient in relation to time.

It is more efficient to provide the teacher with a profile of the student's strengths and weaknesses prior to first attendance. At Rampton Hospital such a profile is compiled through an assessment process which, although time-consuming in itself, is comprehensive and efficient in providing relevant information on which to base educational planning for meeting individual needs.

The assessment process is based on the principle that higher order levels of educational attainment or mental processes should be assessed first, the presumption being that adequacy at a particular level is an indication that lower order skills (or units of knowledge) have been acquired in reaching this level. A similar strategy for assessing problems associated with reading was suggested by K. Weddell (Weddell, 1970). With care in its application this strategy is time-saving and loses nothing in the way of efficiency.

Care involves not always accepting previously recorded information about mentally disordered patients at face value. For example it may be recorded that a patient had before his mental illness an 'O' level in English. Although now recovering from his illness it is apparent that his current level of functioning in English has been affected markedly by his mental disorder. In extreme cases it has been observed for example that the ability to comprehend what has been read is almost non-existent. That is, his mechanical ability remains intact but the ability to comprehend has diminished or even been lost.

As a principle of the assessment process it is fundamental to consider the feelings of the person being tested. It is considered, therefore, of great importance to establish a relationship between tester and patient before the presentation of formal test items. At Rampton Hospital this is done by interviewing the patient at the first meeting without any intention of carrying out formal testing or letting it be known that the assessor is in fact observing (observations are recorded later) the patient. If rapport is achieved, then subsequent meetings will include the presentation of tests. It is essential that any one period of assessment should not be too prolonged or there could be a reduction in the quality of responses.

Table 1 Initial Assessment Stages

Stage	Procedure
1	Previous history e.g. medical records consulted
2	Structured Interview
3	Formal assessment of attainments in basic education
4	Initial Education Report and recommendations on educational placement
5	Diagnostic assessments

Table 1 shows the outline of the initial assessment procedure in the education department. Corresponding to the stages of assessment are standardised record forms on which all observations and recordings are made.

Medical records are the main source of reference for Stage 1, although occasionally the previous institution in which the patient stayed sends an educational report. This is most likely to happen if the patient is transferred from prison. As well as routine information, note is made of physical, perceptual and mental disabilities, previous education and employment and social circumstances.

The aims of the structured interview, Stage 2, are threefold. The first purpose is to familiarise the patient with what the education department has to offer. Secondly, for the teacher to decide on a recommendation for educational placement at a level which meets the patient's most pressing needs. Finally, if the patient is reluctant to attend school to improve his basic educational attainments, the teacher tries to convince him of the benefits the placement would make in preparing him for life in the outside community. The interview is structured, and relevant information and observations are recorded on standardised forms. Although the interviewer is working to a structure, his presentation is informal, trying to give the patient a sense of ease and personal security. At the commencement of the interview the teacher introduces himself and something of the education department's work, and asks (according to circumstances) the patient to respond to general questions about the weather, news, his health etc. The patient is then asked about his previous education. This includes schools attended, attainments, examination successes, attendance and problems. If it is clear at this stage of the interview that the patient has a satisfactory level of basic education, he is then asked about his interests and his ambitions in relation to further education. A report is then compiled and sent to the patient's

41

responsible medical officer. This report is discussed at the patient's initial case conference. In satisfying himself that the patient has a satisfactory level of basic education the interviewer relies mainly on the evidence of past educational and occupational experience, public examination results and the quality of the student's contribution to the interview.

For those who have not demonstrated a satisfactory level of basic education the interview proceeds. The patient is asked about his reading: Can he read? What does he read? When did he last read a newspaper? What difficulties does he have in reading etc?

It has been recognised since the inception of the idea of a structured interview that a question and answer technique would allow the patient the opportunity to present an unrealistic profile of his reading ability. This has always been acceptable for two main reasons. First, his own opinion of his ability can be checked by the observations of other disciplines and by the certainty that he will be given a reading test before the initial report is prepared. Secondly, confirmation that a patient is being unrealistic about his abilities is very valuable information for the teacher if the patient is eventually placed on a basic education course. This point is discussed more fully below.

Writing is next dealt with in a manner similar to that employed for reading. Questions are directed to the skills of letter writing, form filling, and personalised items such as writing one's address and signature. The patient's ability to handle money and time is then assessed using the same technique.

During the interview the teacher makes observations which will enable him to fill in two further sections of the interview, namely, language and 'attitude' during the interview. In the area of language, note is made of speech impediments, echolalia or aphasic tendencies. Additionally the fluency and the sense of responses is assessed. The patient's attitude is examined in two main areas. Firstly, how far is he co-operative or helpful in the interview, and secondly, what his attitude is to the interviewer.

The patient's motivation at this time is not easy to estimate. Nevertheless it is felt important to make some observation on it. Two strategies are used which should be seen as two inter-dependent parts of a whole, and not separate entities. In one the patient is asked if he is keen to attend classes, and if he answers positively, what reasons does he give for this. His replies are then balanced against the conclusion the interviewer has reached from his observations of the patient throughout the interview. This comparison between what the patient says and what the interviewer observes is important, for contradictions are not infrequent. The patient, for example, says he is interested in education and yet the interviewer senses this is not a genuine response, knowing that all to often a patient will follow an institutional pattern in concurring with the system; that is, if it seems to the patient that he is expected to be interested then he will state his interest. The converse can also occur where the patient appears extremely co-operative and eager and then states he is not interested in education. The patient's response in such cases could be based, in part, on his previous negative experience during his time at school. He has an awareness of his inadequacy, but his contact with education has been so traumatic that he cannot see circumstances would be any different in the Hospital's education department. The observations made by the interviewer are important in sustaining the belief that the patient would like to learn and hence providing the basis for a process of gentle persuasion which aims to convince the patient that education in the department is different from his previous experience and worth a try.

The most recent addition to the sections in the structure of the educational interview is a brief note of the patient's mental state during the interview. This description can be no more than the expression of an opinion that the patient either acted and responded within the boundaries of normal acceptable behaviour or that there was evidence of thought disorder. If the latter is expressed, then the findings of the interviewer are invalid for educational purposes but may prove useful to the clinical team.

Although the three main reasons for the interview were given above, there is now a need following the description of the interview to expand on its value.

The interview strategy provides the opportunity for a trusting relationship to be established between the patient and the education department representative. Experience has shown that if formal testing is introduced too soon in the assessment procedure, that is before a patient is ready to face the stress of the situation, there is a chance relationships will be strained. If the questions put to the patient are too objective, resulting in a high level of incorrect responses, there is a danger of highlighting inadequacies at a time when there has been insufficient time for a trusting relationship based on mutual respect to have ripened. It is generally accepted that individuals can be very upset if the assessment procedure is presented with little sensitivity or appreciation of personal feelings. Therefore, great care is taken by the interviewer not to be put in a position where he has to state the patient is wrong.

The interview may also produce information about the level of realism which the patient presents regarding his educational development. This is most important in those cases where a patient over-estimates his ability. Those that do this have sound reasons for doing so. They have to make a pretence that they are as capable as any other person in order to preserve their self-esteem. Without the ability to project an air of competence and confidence they would have even more serious difficulties in adjusting to the demands of living within society and adjusting to its expectations.

The pretence of competence is, therefore, a defence mechanism which helps a patient maintain stability in the face of pressures produced by communal living. He has to conform to certain norms, and although his detention in a special hospital is an indication he has not been entirely successful, there is evidence to suggest he has continued to project an image of competence which in reality has little substance. His front of competence in a wide range of skills is a facade (Bennett, 1976: 27). This facade can be easily breached by those teachers or psychologists who require to know the true level of attainment or ability. The process used by these professions for this purpose can be extremely distressful to the patient. Hence there is a real need before Stage 3, that of formal testing, is carried out for the professional to be aware of those patients who, it is suspected, over-estimate their abilities. The initial interview used by the Rampton Hospital education department is very useful in identifying such patients. As such it signals a need for extreme caution and sensitivity in applying tests of attainment.

One of the most extreme cases of a patient over-estimating his abilities will give some indication of the problem. In 1973 the education department was asked by a charge nurse to see 'Peter S'. This was in the days before our initial assessment procedure had been fully developed. Peter had asked to do 'O' levels in English. His request seemed reasonable to ward staff, for he spent a great deal of time reading and writing. Ward staff had been unable to discuss in any detail with Peter what he wanted to do, but a glance at his written work showed a well-formed hand.

It was quickly established in our interview with Peter that he was certainly not an 'O' level candidate. Although he gave the impression of being articulate, much of what he said comprised of stock phrases and common patterns of response. His hand writing was very expressive but what he had written had been copied directly from the texts of library books. It was this ability to reproduce textual material from printed sources in a flowing and well-controlled hand that was most impressive. It had certainly proved a useful skill in presenting Peter to the world as being reasonably intelligent, to those who were only casually interested in his academic attainments. In reality this proved to be his one major educational attainment. He could not read one word of the many books he had borrowed. Neither could he write anything from memory – even his name or signature were beyond him. His expensive watch was purely ornamental, for he could not tell the time. Most staggering of all was his inability to use money, for many patients have, for practical purposes, a comparitively higher attainment in using money than other basic education skills.

Peter was extremely anxious we should not make his deficiencies widely known. It was extremely stressful for him to consider that both staff and his fellow patients might know his attainments were no better than the 'noddies' (severely mentally handicapped) whom he so despised.

It was to his credit that Peter eventually agreed to attend a basic education group five mornings a week. Trust and confidence both in the teacher and interpersonally took months to develop. Consequently progress in the first year was slow. Reading aloud was a trial, as skill, or lack of it, is easily observable by third persons. It took a considerable time before his suspicions of being watched were overcome and he accepted that his fellow students were truly dis-interested in his attempts.

Peter made good progress in basic education. However on discharge he considered we had failed him for his reading was not yet fluent.

Following the interview session the assumptions made on the placement of patients on the appropriate level of basic education are tested out in Stage 3 of the initial assessment procedure by the application of relevant formal tests and assessments (Table 1).

There are many tests available for the assessment of reading ability, plus approaches which evaluate reading skill without the use of such formal measures. In assessing the level of reading development of patients at Rampton two tests are used: the Burt Rearranged Word Reading Test to assess mechanical reading ability (Burt, 1976) and the G.A.P. Reading Comprehension Test (McLeod and Unwin, 1970).

Both tests are useful in that they give us a fairly accurate relative measure of reading development expressed in terms of reading age, and yet can be applied with a minimum of expenditure in staff time.

All patients considered for basic education levels I, II and III will be assessed on the two reading tests. In practice however those with a reading age of less than seven years on the Burt test will be unable to do the G.A.P. test.

Perhaps surprisingly the results from using the Burt test have been predictive as to which level of basic education the patient should start on. It has been found that those patients with reading ages less than nine are the same individuals which the interview procedure has identified as being in need of basic education level I or II. On the other hand, while a few patients of reading age nine years and above may require one of the two first levels of education, the majority meet the requirements of level III.

Although the Burt and G.A.P. tests are used to assess the formal development of reading, a number of subsequent assessment items attempt to gauge the functional application of reading skill in specific areas of social competence. Teaching staff at Rampton Hospital lay greater stress on the functional development of reading, in contrast to the normal practice of formal development of reading through the application of a hierarchical system of skills.

Once the Burt and GA.P. tests have been applied to all patients being considered for basic education, the next stage is to examine other areas of basic education. Those patients who are considered for basic education levels I and II will be given the communication section of the Progress Assessment Chart 2 (Gunzburg, 1974). Patients with higher attainment will complete the Rampton Basic Studies Assessment Tests (B.S.A.T.).

At the end of Stage 2 – structured interview, and Stage 3 – formal assessment of attainments in basic education, Stage 4 of the Initial Assessment Procedure is implemented (Table 1) for patients being considered for basic education. Stage 4 consists of preparing a report which is sent to the patient's responsible medical officer and his ward. In principle this report serves the same function as that described above for patients not in need of basic education.

The main sections of the report consist of personal details, educational and related social history (if available), results of formal testing, interviews and assessments, summary and recommendations.

The main recommendations consist of advice on educational placing. Where basic education is required the level – I, II or III – is stated. Additionally, where the patient has requested other subjects, or it is felt by the reporter that other subjects would meet the patient's needs, these are recommended.

The report is discussed at the patient's initial case planning conference. The conference receives and considers reports from all disciplines concerned with the patient's treatment and rehabilitation. The needs of the patient as presented by each discipline are discussed, thus providing opportunity to extend and elaborate on the information available. The patient is also invited to give his views, and with increasing frequency relatives are also asked to attend.

Although a report of the case conference is compiled and sent to each of the disciplines concerned, the education representative is asked to note anything of relevance which is brought out during discussion.

The conference ends with agreements on the immediate needs of the patient. This includes which ward would be most suitable to his needs, his chemo-therapeutic requirements, establishment of contacts with relatives and social services through the social work department, which work area would be most suitable in the occupation department, educational placement, and possible psychological investigations and treatment. Unless the patient is particularly disturbed or mentally ill, a recommendation for basic education is accepted by case conferences. The attainment of a satisfactory level of basic education is generally seen as a pressing need.

Information acquired about a patient through the Stages 1 to 4 of the initial assessment procedure assists in making decisions about educational placement. This information is also invaluable, in that it provides teachers with knowledge essential to the process of developing individualised learning programmes for each student. Nevertheless for those patients who are recommended for levels I and II basic education the information is insufficient for this purpose. A further stage of assessment is carried out: that of diagnostic assessment shown as Stage 5 in Table 1.

To those not familiar with the education of the mentally disordered, this depth and extent of assessment may appear extravagant in both time and energy. However Gunzburg (Gunzburg, 1968: preface) is in no doubt about the necessity of individual assessment for the mentally handicapped child.

"Drawing up a balance sheet of assets and deficiencies in an individual child may help the teacher to avoid frittering away well-meaning efforts on a pale imitation of 'normal academic education'."

The experience of teaching staff at Rampton Hospital indicates that Gunzburg's observation is equally applicable to the mentally disordered of all ages.

In reading, a large proportion of patients on the basic education courses levels I and II are unlikely to reach a high level of literacy. It is therefore important to know which of the most important words they are likely to come across they can read. At Rampton two lists of words are considered essential in achieving a level of functional literacy. The first list consists of fifty-two social vocabulary words e.g. TOILETS, EXIT. The second list is the 'Key Words to Literacy' (McNally, 1968). Words on this list are particularly important, for they have been identified as being the words most frequently in common use in reading texts. Early incorporation of these words into a reader's sight vocabulary is considered vital (McNally and Murray, 1962). Both lists are applied as diagnostic tests.

Results from the application of the two word lists give a clearer indication of the immediate functional reading needs of the patient than those obtained through the Burt or GA.P. tests described above. Nevertheless a substantial number of students have been found to have acquired a sizable sight vocabulary but are stunted in their reading ability by an inability to tackle new words. Words in context which are not familiar can be guessed at or synthesised through a process of blending constituent sounds. The latter process is known as a phonic approach to reading while the former is called informed contextual guessing. To test a patient's ability in the phonic approach, a word synthesis test is applied.

The word synthesis test is important in providing an indication of a patient's current ability to go beyond the acquisition of a sight vocabulary to a stage where he is able to make sense from graphically represented phonic units. Without this facility and the additional crucial psycho-linguistic 'informed contextual guessing', reading will stick at the individual's ability to memorize words by the "look and say" method. From experience at Rampton Hospital of mentally handicapped and dull-average patients this means in practical terms being restricted to the reading of approximately two hundred words.

The Progress Assessment Chart 2, although assessing money and time skills, does not specifically identify basic number skills. In Stage 5 of the initial assessment procedure the following areas are tested:

A. Mental Arithmetic.　　　Addition (1) Add single to single digit numbers,
　　　　　　　　　　　　　　　　　(2) Add single to double digit numbers.
　　　　　　　　　　　Subtraction – same levels as addition.
B. Counting (1) units, (2) tens, (3) hundreds, (4) thousands.
C. Written Arithmetic.　　　Addition (1) Add single columns
　　　　　　　　　　　　　　　　(2) Add double columns not carrying 10's.
　　　　　　　　　　　　　　　　(3) Add double columns carrying 10's.
　　　　　　　　　　　Subtraction (1) Take away single numbers.
　　　　　　　　　　　　　　　　(2) Take away double numbers – no
　　　　　　　　　　　　　　　　　　'borrowing'.
　　　　　　　　　　　　　　　　(3) Take away double numbers
　　　　　　　　　　　　　　　　　　'borrowing'.
D. Place Value (1) units, (2) tens, (3) hundreds, (4) thousands.

All the tests and assessments described so far under Stage 5 have been concerned with obtaining information about patients' attainments. They are extensions to the tests carried out in Stage 3. However, the attainments are qualitatively much lower, and the necessity to use the tests with patients is indicative of minimal levels of development. Therefore the patients have within their lives failed to learn what would appear to be very simple skills. Many theories have been put forward to explain why individuals do not learn. One of the most fundamental of these is related to the observation:

> "that some children entering school at five years of age have an underlying psycho-motor organisation not favouring the acquisition of consistent symbolic learning".
>
> (Thompson & Norton, undated)

This statement is specific to young children, but it is evident from work with the mentally disordered at Rampton Hospital that the problem can exist in adolescence and adulthood. If an individual's psycho-motor organisation is incomplete, then his potential for learning is impaired.

H. C. Gunzburg, in relating intelligence to reading, stated:

> "although it may be a reasonable generalisation to say that people with I.Q. between 55 and 69 should be able to read, there may be individuals within the group in whom an inability to read may be due to a specific factor not connected with intelligence".
>
> (Gunzburg, 1968: 27)

If the generalisation expressed by Gunzburg has foundation, the responsibility of an education department in a special hospital is to examine further the possible causes of not only reading failure but failure in other areas of the basic education curriculum, most importantly number, writing and language.

If the problem in the past has been a lack of opportunity or a failure, for whatever reason, to take advantage of opportunities for learning, then it may be reasonable to begin the process of developing basic educational ATTAINMENTS. However, one cannot be sure that this is the case for those patients exhibiting a very low level of attainment. The possibility cannot be ruled out that the reason for failure is related to other specific factors connected with the psycho-motor organisation of the individual. A failure to identify and remediate these factors would ensure that the individual is once again frustrated in his attempt to learn basic social and life skills. The damage to his already handicapped personality could be traumatic. It is necessary therefore within the diagnostic testing to include assessments which assist in identifying weaknesses in the psycho-motor-organisation of the individual.

Since 1974 it has been the policy to assess all patients with limited attainments in those specific areas which appear to be necessary prerequisites to the learning of reading, number, writing and spoken language skills. Patients whose reading attainment is almost nil are assessed on tests of visual discrimination and visual sequential memory. Without an adequate level of development in these visual areas it is highly unlikely that a patient can make progress in extending his sight vocabulary. Concurrently 'shape' recognition of words is reinforced through a graphical reproduction. It is therefore important to test visual copying ability in tracing or carrying out other basic hand/eye coordination tasks. The ability to progress reading ability using a phonic approach requires sound visual development in recognising letters and their sequential arrangement. 'Phonic readiness' is also highly dependent on the individual's ability to hear and discriminate sounds, remember the order in which they are heard and finally blend them into words. Word synthesis, recognition and identification of letter sounds and names, ability to blend sounds and short term memory of sounds are areas which require assessment in part or whole if patients have problems in developing a phonic approach to reading.

Gaps in the psycho-motor organisation of the individual highlighted by our assessment procedure have implications for the curriculum. The deficiencies in abilities must be given priority in designing relevant individualised basic education programmes.

Until 1980 the education department's own diagnostic strategy was used. It is based mainly on the work of A. E. Tansley (Tansley, 1972) and organised according to the structure for assessment designed by K. Weddell (1970) noted above, where higher order skills are always tested before lower order ones. Since that date its use has been replaced by the Aston Index (Newton, M. J. and Thomson, M. E., undated). The Index is produced commercially and presumably is widely used in special education. The main reason for changing to the Index was the possibility of comparing results obtained from Rampton Hospital patients with results from other institutions. There is however the possibility that the education department will revert to its own system in the near future, as experience is tending to indicate that the system is more suited to its requirements.

The identification of individual needs by a process of assessment is a major factor affecting the structure of the curriculum at Rampton Hospital. Without such a procedure it is highly likely that the organisation and content of the curriculum would be quite different to that described in Chapter IV. Though the education department has developed in such a way that most emphasis is put on basic education and associated life skills, it has not been unmindful of other needs which patients may have. As indicated earlier, some patients have a need to follow academic study. Physical recreation and creative activity are areas which many patients want to take part in. These needs are met by the range of activities described in Chapter IV.

Task Related Areas (c) Security

Special hospitals are maximum security establishments. Nevertheless as patients improve in their mental states they are moved through a system of ward changes from a state of extremely high security to one where the security is still high but recognises that patients will soon be transferred to open hospitals, hostels or the community. In the least secure parts of the hospital, the pre-discharge areas, patients remain under surveillance, and on shopping trips to town or other organised visits are always escorted.

The security factor has a major effect on the organisation and effectiveness of the curriculum. In addition to the problem of punctuality the teachers' task is frustrated in several areas.

One of the major dilemmas facing teachers is how to prepare patients for life outside by the development of life, social and communication skills in an establishment which bears little resemblance to conditions in the community at large. From the point of view of motivating students this is a major stumbling block. Outside life seems so remote that many students have great difficulty in appreciating that what they are being asked to learn has any relevance to them.

Teaching is also affected in that security reduces the opportunity to present learning tasks in normal situations. Role play can be valuable in reducing the effects of such restrictions. However without occasional recourse to real-life experience there is a tendency for this strategy to become tedious and unmeaningful. For example shopping for dummy goods even using real money has a limit of usefulness if one is not able to reinforce that task by making real purchases in a shop and using what is bought.

Security has an inhibiting effect on the motivation of students and teaching opportunities. Other disciplines are also affected in a similar manner in their treatment processes. This does not mean however that, because of security, treatment in the hospital is of no value. It can be argued that without a vigorous approach to treatment by hospital disciplines the effects on patients of a maximum security regime would be so devastating that there would be little chance of ever rehabilitating them back into the community. Conditions for rehabilitation and resocialisation are far from ideal in a top-security establishment but a highly dedicated and skilled staff representing all disciplines is capable of mitigating the worst effects of security.

Security can also pose a problem for teachers which normally they will only have previously encountered in being assessed on their teaching practice as students or probationary teachers. This is the stress encountered in being observed by a person who is not directly involved in the teaching experience. All teaching staff have to become used to teaching in their area within the presence of observers, in this case nursing staff, who are present to maintain security. There are occasions where the already very complicated teaching task is further aggravated by this presence.

It is agreed by teaching staff that the situation is at its most stimulating and free from tension when nursing staff assist in the learning process. Experience has also shown that where nurses are involved in the actual process of teaching there is a higher degree of security than when they are passive onlookers.

Task Related Areas (d) Inter-disciplinary Co-operation

Although strides have been made in furthering inter-disciplinary communication as witnessed above in the description of case conferences and nurses and teachers working together on joint ventures, and in the work of the Vocational Preparation Unit, there are still instances of lack of consultation and planning in making decisions regarding individual patient treatment.

One of the most irritating occurrences to teaching staff of a breakdown in communication is when patients are taken off classes without prior consultation of their teachers. There have been several examples of this kind of withdrawal at times when the patients concerned have been making good progress both in behaviour and attainment.

A further source of bewilderment is when enthusiastic staff of other disciplines set up treatment programmes which duplicate activities carried out in the education department. The education staff recognise that the staff concerned have seen a need for such programmes and support the motivation for their actions. Teachers however feel that far more effective use of resources, skill and knowledge would result if such ventures were discussed with education staff prior to their implementation.

An attempt to consult in this manner should not be seen as a ploy by the education staff to gain control of the project. Teaching staff have always recognised that the problem of developing communication skills in the patient population is so extensive that they cannot tackle it on their own. They have always acknowledged that nursing staff in particular have a major part to play in developing communication skills. Nevertheless success depends on a common policy. A fragmented approach is not only ineffective: it could result in a number of teaching methods being used for the same purpose at the same time, which would result not in enlightenment but in confusion. Nurses, occupation officers, and teachers, should work in harmony creating an atmosphere for the reinforcement of skill in areas where the opportunity arises for development. It is crucial that learning be reinforced and not merely duplicated. Duplication ignores inter-disciplinary co-operation whereas reinforcement is the fruit of it.

Task Related Areas (e) The Nature of Mental Disorder

Earlier in the chapter it was stressed most forcefully that the development of the curriculum and its effectiveness was dependent on the assessment of individual needs. It was inferred that the department was presented with a most difficult task in coming to terms with the very complex personalities of its students. Although mention was made of the three main classifications of mental disorder – mental illness, mental handicap and psychopathic disorder, it was made clear that educational planning depended more on taking account of levels of attainment and potential ability than on the existing mental state or classification of patients. Nevertheless experience has shown that though the basic organisation should be drawn up within the framework of an educational model which should eventually see an increase in the competence of patients, other factors cannot be ignored. One factor which cannot be ignored which seems to have played a major part in the lives of many patients and is contributory to their disturbed behaviour is that of cultural and social deprivation. This was a concept seen by the Schools Council (Working Party No. 27, 1970: 23-32) as being so stunting to the development of secondary school children that educators should not only recognise its potency but should organise the curriculum to compensate for its worst effects. This means having, in addition to the aim of competence, two further aims, those of confidence and co-operation as the foci of planning.

Although defining objectives to meet the aims of confidence and co-operation are not so obvious as they are for the aim of competence, the education department at Rampton in meeting individual needs has been reasonably successful in achieving these aims. Two psychiatrists have in fact commented that they feel the social experience provided by the education department is extremely valuable in combating the effects of social maladjustment, and place this as a priority even before the development of competence in skill and knowledge. Teachers see the three aims as being interdependent – there can be no development of competence, unless trust and confidence and co-operation within the learning process are nurtured. Conversely the development of confidence and co-operation depends on success achieved in increasing competence.

Cultural and social deprivation leading to severe maladjustment has therefore been a feature of the lives of a large number of patients and has affected the way the education department at Rampton organises its curriculum. Until recently this factor dominated the affective aspect of the work of teachers. However, the comparatively recent change whereby Rampton ceased to be a hospital mainly for the mentally handicapped and 'low grade' psychopath to a position where these groups are now out-numbered by the mentally ill has indicated a need to re-examine the position.

One of the main organisational features of the education department until 1984 was its 'open plan' arrangement. The education department building had previously housed the weaving occupation workshop. When it was handed over to the education department in 1972 it was decided not to compartmentalise the space available. The reason for this was that an 'open plan' arrangement would not preclude the implementation of individualised learning programmes while at the same time preserving the opportunity to create an atmosphere promoting social intercourse in the basic education sessions. Such an arrangement was eminently suitable for our students at this time. They were in general either diagnosed as mentally handicapped or psychopathic of low ability. They presented features of gross under-socialisation and poor social competence.

Rae Than (Than, 1982), a member of the teaching staff, became increasingly aware that the education department's open plan arrangement did not appear to suit a number of patients placed on basic education groups who were suffering from mental illness. As she was aware that the number of mentally ill patients was increasing and the numbers of those with other classifications decreasing, she was concerned about the apparent incompatibility of mentally ill patients and the department's open plan arrangement.

In a study presented as part of her studies for an Advanced Diploma in Special Education she compared the behaviour and educational progress of a group of mentally ill patients with those of a group of mentally handicapped. Although she found no significant differences between the two groups on the variables she examined, her experience convinced her that the open plan arrangement was not suitable for mentally ill students. Her opinion was supported by most of the teaching staff who had also observed how intolerant a number of mentally ill were of noise and movement.

A great deal of discussion followed on whether the education department was justified in asking hospital management to reconstruct the education building to a standard which would meet the needs of the majority of its students. That the management was approached and agreed to the proposition made by the department is manifest in the structural alterations made in 1985. The 'new' classrooms would appear to meet the needs of all students: the mentally ill are more composed and less distracted while the mentally handicapped appear to have adequate opportunity for social interaction through paired and group activities and during breaks.

How far a teacher needs to know about the aetiology of mental disorders would seem debatable. Students are recommended for education, and their needs in this respect, as far as teaching staff are concerned, are paramount. Nevertheless, while keeping this fact to the fore-front in planning the curriculum content it has to be recognised that staff must be as fully aware as is possible of the affective side of their student's personality. This is merely repeating a truth which is applicable to teaching anywhere. In a special hospital the behaviour of a student may be a symptom of previous adverse social experiences or of mental illness. Teachers must be capable of understanding behaviour which impedes or interrupts learning. For this they do not require the detailed knowledge of a psychiatrist but rather an acumen for detailed observation, the ability to foster trusting teacher-student relationships and the foresight to seek advice when a problem appears intractable. The decision to abandon the 'open plan' arrangement in the education department for a more closed physical system is an example of teaching staff coming to terms with and understanding the affective needs of students with varying degrees of mental disorder.

Summary

The task of an education department in a special hospital is complex. It is suggested that it is important for the education department to be aware that those responsible for special hospitals and disciplines working in special hospitals recognise that education has a meaningful part to play in the attainment of treatment aims and policies. The education department has two main tasks. Its first duty is to facilitate the process whereby through active treatment patients attain a higher level of personal social competence. Secondly it must be aware of its potential as a force in the personal development of individuals, providing opportunities for such development to be nurtured. Associated with this second duty is an awareness that the provision of a wide range of educational activities reduces the risk of institutionalisation for patients.

Areas of activity and knowledge affecting the implementation of the tasks identified for the education department are discussed. It is stressed that the education department carries out a thorough initial assessment process. The process produces information crucial to the formulation and implementation of individualised learning programmes. In general, security depresses opportunity for learning and consequently adversely affects education. Inter-disciplinary co-operation is a major factor in improving success rate but is not always easy to achieve in a multidisciplinary institution. It affects the task of education as it does those of other disciplines. Finally the nature of mental disorder is shown to produce problems not easy to resolve in attempting to come to terms with the tasks facing the education department.

Chapter IV

THE CURRICULUM

"No other educational institutions are concerned with students who have
such a wide range of ability and personality problems and the teachers
are faced with a most exacting task".

(Boynton, 1980: 97)

The curriculum at Rampton Hospital reflects the need to provide
educational opportunities for all students. Additionally it gives recognition to the need to assist the hospital in meeting its primary aims of
treatment. In attempting to meet these needs the current structure of
the education department's curriculum can be identified as having
developed five areas of educational provision; these are: 1. basic
education, 2. vocational preparation, 3. perceptuo – motor and primary
communication programmes, 4. general and academic education, and
5. leisure/recreational activities. There is a possible alternative to this
structure by classifying activities according to the main tasks identified
for the department in the previous chapter. Activities such as basic
education and basic cookery classes would fall in the area of social
competence, while weight training or photography would be placed
under personal development. However, as all subjects have the
potential for personal development or reducing the effects of the
institution, reference to the alternative structure could require an
overuse of qualification.

The description of a curriculum includes integral features other than
subjects and/or activities. Teaching staff, their competence and attitudes, the resources they have available, and their methods of teaching
are major issues in any accurate representation of the curriculum.

The following description of the educational curriculum at Rampton
attempts to give a comprehensive account of those factors which appear
to feature most in its structure and implementation.

Basic Education

More than half the physical and teaching resources of the education
department at Rampton Hospital are utilised by the basic education
programme. This provision reflects a situation within the hospital
population whereby there has always been and continues to exist a large
number of patients who have severe problems with literacy and
numeracy, and even at a more fundamental level, with speech.

58

The organisation of the basic education programme at three levels has been a development. Originally there was only a single basic education provision, but a greater awareness of the problem and the necessity to allocate resources according to greatest need resulted in a more differentiated structure.

Table 2 Organisation of Basic Education

Level	Number of groups	Number of sessions	Length of sessions	Total weekly hours	Total students (max)
I	6	5 mornings	2½ hours	12½	48
II	4	3 aftns.	2 hours	6	32
III	6	2 aftns.	2 hours	4	60

(a) *Level 1 Basic Education – Context and Structure*

Table 2 shows that in terms of total weekly hours, the level I programme has the greatest allocation. The reason for this is that selected students have been identified as having the severest degrees of underfunction in communication skills. Their educational need is greatest, and consequently relatively more time is allocated to the remediation process.

The structure of the programme for level I is based on the Communication section of the Progress Assessment Chart 2, usually referred to as the P.A.C. 2, (Gunzburg, H., 1974). The author of the P.A.C. 2, H. C. Gunzburg, was the earliest pioneer in Britain of the modern approach to the social education of the mentally handicapped. In the P.A.C. 2 he is concerned with the assessment of social educational skills which are relevant and within the learning capabilities of adult mentally handicapped people. He organises these skills under four headings: self-help, occupations, socialisation and communication. The education department has the resources to make its most effective contribution to the development of those skills identified by Gunzburg under communication.

In the previous chapter, in the description of the initial assessment procedure, it was stated that patients identified through the application of the P.A.C. 2 of having deficiencies in communication skills were referred to the education department for assistance with their problems. The task of the teachers is to help such patients acquire deficient skills. Thus the P.A.C. 2 provides parameters for the construction of the level I curriculum.

Consideration has been given to a restructure of level I using as a basis alternative structures to Gunzburg's P.A.C. There have been an increasing number of these structures, particularly those such as the 'Copewell System' (Whelan, Speake & Strickland, 1984) developed at the Hester Adrian Centre, Manchester. The department finally rejected a departure from Gunzburg and opted for refinements of his basic structure carried out by teaching staff as an organised department curriculum project.

The communication section of the P.A.C. 2 consists of five areas: language, money, time, writing and reading. In each area there are six assessment items. For the mentally handicapped the correct response to each of these assessment items is dependent on the development of a number of inter-related skills. The identification of these inter-related skills has been a major objective of the department and has contributed to the refinement of the P.A.C. 2 communication section. Once identified, an attempt is made to arrange these skills in an hierarchy of difficulty leading to the ultimate attainment of the relevant P.A.C. 2 item. Each skill is defined as an objective to be attained. A list of objectives relating to the P.A.C. 2 item is called a check list. Each of the P.A.C. 2 assessment items now has a check list of skills which enable the teacher to approach the development of a P.A.C. item step by step. This not only ensures that teaching is relevant and appropriate to need but assists student motivation as each small component of learning is given recognition. Considerable assistance in the compilation of check lists for our basic education course was obtained through consulting the publication of Bender and Valletutti (Bender, M. and Valletutti, 1976).

An example of how the task of attaining the P.A.C. 2 item "Can write his signature in an acceptable way" has been analysed and presented as a checklist of inter-related sub-skills is given as follows:
1. Can trace letters included in his name.
2. Can trace his surname in print.
3. Can trace his Christian name in print.
4. Can trace his signature – cursive writing.
5. Can copy letters in his name.
6. Can copy his surname in print.
7. Can copy his Christian name in print.
8. Can copy his signature – cursive writing.
9. Can reproduce letters included in his name.
10. Can reproduce his surname.

11. Can reproduce his Christian name.
12. Can WRITE his signature in an acceptable way.

It may be evident from the description given of the P.A.C. 2 communication section that its organisation does not follow the usual pattern of developing basic education which is apparent in the school system. In schools, reading is a basic skill, the acquisition of which is imperative if progress in a wide range of subjects is to be acquired. It does not remain skill-specific and is adaptable to numerous learning situations. Reading in this sense for adults who are mentally disordered and/or who have failed many attempts to become competent may not prove totally impossible but it is evident that it is a more realistic strategy to give priority to the acquisition of a reading vocabulary which is specific to immediate social needs.

The reading priority for students in the basic education level I programme is the development of a social sight vocabulary. This follows the order suggested by the P.A.C. 2 in developing literacy. The vocabulary consists of words and signs which are found on notices in public places: the street, bus and railway station, civic, government and commercial offices and shops.

The basic vocabulary in the education department is comprised of fifty-two words. It is extended further up to two hundred words including a number from other important areas. For example common words on forms such as first name, surname, date etc. are included. The first literacy programme for adults 'On the Move' screened by the BBC in 1975 followed a similar structure.

The basic education level I programme, as the description so far indicates, is a clearly defined structure. It concentrates on the five communication skills of language, money, time, writing and reading. Within each area of skill six broad objectives are set. These broad objectives are achieved in attending to items of learning clearly defined in a related check list.

The level I programme includes a further feature. It was recognised at an early stage that a long morning, five days a week, of basic education would prove too demanding for students and could be counter productive if rigidly enforced. Within the week therefore the opportunity is available to take part in other activities as an option. Physical education, swimming, dress-making, soft toy making, art, computer games, music, current affairs, drama etc. have all been available at some time for students to take part in at least two half mornings a week.

These activities are not mere palliatives introduced as a strategy to make the B.E. level I more attractive. They provide opportunity to develop personal qualities which are fundamental to the remediation process. Integral abilities such as visual and auditory perception, hand/eye co-ordination, fine and gross motor skills can be and are improved.

The most recent development in the programme has been the inclusion of art as a compulsory component. Students have one or two hourly sessions a week in the subject. The rationale for making art work an essential feature of the programme stems from the problem of understanding the needs of the increasing number of mentally-ill students. Art can be a medium of communication, and as the education department is fortunate in having a member of staff trained in art therapy his skill can be most useful in interpreting students' work. Coming to an understanding of the student through his art work is a valuable contribution not only to his short term education but to his ultimate rehabilitation. Currently the department is feeling its way in this venture and there is a need to monitor progress.

(b) *Level II Basic Education – Content and Structure*

Basic Education level II structure is identical to the first level. However, it does not include optional activities or art in its programme. The difference between the two levels lies not in structure but in the initial levels of attainment of students. Whereas level I students will be deficient in all P.A.C. 2 communication areas, those on level II will be unsatisfactory in no more than three of the five areas.

(c) *Level III Basic Education (Basic Studies) – Content and Structure*

The Gunzburg P.A.C. 2 was designed to meet the basic educational, social and occupational needs of the mentally handicapped. The assessment items in each area of communication are related to very basic areas of attainment. Even where a student successfully covered all the communication assessment items he would still be at a relatively restricted level of social competence. It was recognised in the early days of the department that a significant proportion of students could meet the demands of the P.A.C. 2 but were still not making full use of their potential and had levels of basic education attainment well below that which is accepted as reasonable. Many of these students were not mentally handicapped and were of average ability. Courses under the heading 'basic studies' were organised to meet the needs of these students.

The main problem in the early days of the programme was the lack of any structure other than that provided by aims defined to improve reading, writing and spelling and arithmetic. There was a tendency for teaching to follow a pattern more clearly suitable for junior education. This was in marked contrast to the basic education level I and II programme, which as described above was specific in dealing with the development of communication skills in order to enhance social competence.

Other than the provision of a reading age and an I.Q. score, teaching staff had little knowledge of each individual student's attainments and abilities when they were placed on classes. Each member of staff made his own decision as to teaching priorities. This produced a situation where the basic studies curriculum in one group was markedly dissimilar to that of another group. While some relevant areas were well covered, others were neglected or even not recognised. It was difficult to monitor individual progress which relied over much on the subjective assessment of teachers.

A structure for the basic education level III course was developed (Bennett, B., 1977: 21-28) with the intention of improving the programme. It was predicted that a suitable structure would produce several benefits. The existence of a common policy would ensure staff were frequently reminded of the need to attend to all priorities included in the structure. Structure would assist the development of a comprehensive assessment procedure providing opportunity for increased accuracy in testing and monitoring progress. Such an assessment procedure would also be valuable to teachers as a yardstick in measuring their teaching efficiency. Improved assessment would facilitate more accurate reports on progress to psychiatrists and other clinical staff. Students would also benefit through knowing what the course required of them. Insight into their own personal development would be facilitated in keeping their own record charts. Finally, although this advantage has not subsequently turned out to be so important, structure would enable those who successfully complete the course to be identified.

The structural content of the basic education level III course (basic studies) was modified in 1980 (Bennett, B., 1980: 378-385) and is under further consideration at the present time. It is defined in terms of assessable objectives and consists of a manual stating the objectives and how they are to be assessed. Basically the structure is in two categories: the first category includes areas of attainment associated with the basic skills of learning i.e. the 3Rs, the second category is concerned with how basic attainments are utilised in life and social skills and also includes areas of useful general knowledge.

The main divisions of category I are writing, reading and arithmetic. Writing is sub-divided into four areas: legibility, functional spelling, developmental spelling, and construction. Reading has two components, accuracy and comprehension, while arithmetic is divided into mental arithmetic, the four number processes up to long division and multiplication, parts of wholes, and metric measurement and calculations. Parts of wholes consist of knowing common fractions i.e. $\frac{1}{3}$, $\frac{1}{6}$, $\frac{1}{2}$, $\frac{1}{4}$, $\frac{1}{5}$, $\frac{1}{10}$, percentages i.e. 5%, 10% et seq. and decimals, and knowing equivalents e.g $\frac{1}{4} = 25\% = 0.25$. Each area has from five to ten specific objectives.

Category II is divided into ten areas of skill or knowledge: Getting a Job, Wages, Budgeting, Savings and Economical Use of Personal Income, Personal Interests and Hobbies, Travel and Transport, Personal Knowledge and Health, Use of Reference Skills.

The emphasis currently placed on each category II area highlights the change in society which has occurred over the past ten years. Whereas originally the skills required for 'Getting a Job' were paramount and Personal Interests and Hobbies were relatively marginal, the current employment situation has brought them much closer together in deciding priorities. The ability to use free time constructively and in a way that enhances personal development would appear to be an essential aim for special hospital patients in a climate of reduced job opportunity.

Though the parameters of the basic education level III course (basic studies) are clearly defined, the content is extensive and challenging. Attendance on the course is restricted to two afternoons a week. Although students can expect to spend years rather than months in special hospitals thus giving them opportunity to attend the education department for long periods of time, there is a feeling than an additional session a week would be beneficial. So far resources have not proved adequate to provide more time.

Vocational Preparation

Vocational Preparation is a concept new to the outside world and it is perhaps surprising to note that an organisation frequently accused of being isolationist and out of date is involved in work related to this concept.

In its constant attempt to meet its aim of improving the social competence of its patients the hospital finally agreed to the establishment of a vocational preparation unit (V.P.U.). The idea for the unit came about from an appraisal of the attempt over many years to establish at the hospital a workshop outside the secure area. The workshop, it was envisaged, would provide realistic work-training in an actual factory setting with procedures such as clocking on, proper wages, canteen meals etc. being integral features of the organisation. The appraisal indicated that the concept had been outdated by the changes in employment opportunities. Note was taken of recent developments in the community, particularly the work of the Manpower Services Commission (M.S.C.) and the Further Education Unit (F.E.U.) in their education and training programmes for young people. The Youth Opportunities Programme and Youth Training Schemes run by Manpower Services Commission and further education colleges appear to have been catalysts in the development of a new concept, that of Vocational Preparation.

The first stage of Vocational Preparation (V.P.) is its core, which consists of a range of basic essential skills. The education department's reaction to the type of skills listed in the core was to note that what the proponents of V.P. were suggesting was the development of social competence in several key areas, these being basic literacy, numeracy, other communication skills, work orientation, work skills, leisure etc. It was also very evident that if V.P. was applicable to the situation at Rampton the basic core skills could only be developed through the close co-operation of all disciplines. V.P. could therefore emerge as a channel of communication which would be readily understood and appreciated by all disciplines.

The Chief Occupations Officer at Rampton, Mr. G. Gavin, considered the idea of a vocational preparation unit as an alternative to the outside workshop as being in the best interests of patients, providing as it did the opportunity to associate the hospital rehabilitation programme with current developments in society. Patients identified for discharge in the near future could be brought together in the Vocational Preparation Unit; they would be thoroughly reassessed at this stage in three areas viz (1) work preparation, (2) communication and education and (3) personal development in health, interpersonal relationships and leisure. Priority needs in the three areas would be established for each individual. The remaining time spent in the hospital would be used to see that the meeting of these needs was attempted.

It was agreed that the three disciplines involved daily in activities which were part of the overall structure of any Vocational Preparation package should staff the unit. Although staff should work as a team, in many areas of activities it was appreciated that, in general, occupations staff would be responsible for work preparation objectives, education staff for communication and education objectives and nursing staff for objectives related to personal development in health, personal relationships and leisure.

It is difficult to organise vocational preparation at Rampton other than at the first stage of its conceptual framework i.e. that of developing essential core skills. Despite limitations of opportunity for occupations staff an attempt is made to meet the demands of the second stage i.e. that of providing experience in a wider number of jobs. Nevertheless the third stage, that of training in a specific area of work, has proved to be unrealistic. This does not invalidate the work being attempted in the V.P. unit. If the hospital does all in its power to ensure that patients leave having utilised their potential to further their personal development in the three areas of the basic core skills, the chances of subsequent rehabilitation and resettlement being successful are enhanced.

In essence the work of the member of the education department working full-time in the V.P.U. is to maximise the time left available before a student leaves the hospital. The teacher has to decide on priority needs while taking into consideration how realistic it is to meet certain needs given a comparatively short time scale. His programme has therefore to be strictly relevant and attainable in the time available. In resource terms he has the assistance of another member of the teaching staff four half mornings a week.

A recent review of the V.P.U. by the Head of the Psychology Department, Mr. M. Lee-Evans, confirmed what a number of hospital staff had anticipated at the time, that the V.P.U. was established. Lee-Evans reported that V.P.U. staff were faced with meeting an inordinate number of needs. Their task was being complicated by the effort to tackle deficiencies in patients' social competence which should and could have been remedied earlier in their stay in the hospital.

This observation has major implications for all hospital disciplines. However, a thorough examination by each discipline of its aims, objectives and policies will not of itself solve the problem. The issue is related directly to the hospital's ability to formulate and direct a policy which involves the close co-ordination and co-operation of all disciplines involved in the process of resocialisation. No single patient's needs can be effectively tackled by one discipline. One discipline may have the task of seeing that a skill is taught or acquired, but other disciplines should be aware of the need to reinforce and nurture the skill's development. A team approach in the process of resocialisation would appear to be the only way offering a chance of success. Achieving it is a considerable task. However the formulation of a taxonomy of identified needs stating each discipline's possible contribution and responsibility to the attainment of every need could indicate to members of staff their own particular responsibilities in the process of resocialisation. Awareness of one's own and of members' of other disciplines responsibilities in the meeting of identified needs might prove the basis for more positive multi-disciplinary co-operation.

Perceptuo-Motor and Primary Communication Programmes

In outlining the task of the education department in Chapter III the nursing staff's contribution to the establishment of the perceptuo-motor activities programme was acknowledged. It was stated that the programme was set up for severely mentally handicapped patients for whom the classroom activities were inappropriate.

Currently Rampton Hospital cares for forty patients having this severe degree of handicap. In attending the gymnasium for the perceptuo-motor programme they are divided into four groups. Each group attends at least twice a week. The sessions last between one and two hours. A great deal of the work is individualised, consequently although session times are long students are not under constant pressure.

Basically the aims of the programme are to reduce the student's high level of dependency and to improve his quality of life.

In a short description it is difficult to give justice to the skill of those who devise the programme's activities and the framework in which they work. Basically students are taught activities and skills that will develop personal control and impulsiveness and increase their ability to attend to their environment. Additionally the aim is to activate arousal and awareness of self, not only as a person with arms, legs, face etc. but also finding one's self in different places and situations e.g. standing, sitting, lying, rolling and moving by different ways on foot. Training a student to stand on a red square for an increasing length of time not only helps the objective of reducing impulsiveness and increasing attention but can also reinforce his appreciation of the colour – RED, the shape – SQUARE and the position – STANDING. If the square is reduced in size or raised from the floor this facilitates an improvement of balance.

Standing on a square may seem to be a rather restricted activity, but if it is used as a progression to a more useful activity it is justified. Students who have been on the programme for some time can now give sufficient attention to directions that they are able to complete a simple circuit of activities without being distracted.

Understanding oral instructions is a major problem for the severely mentally handicapped. Occasionally this is due to inherent deafness, but in the majority of cases it is a failure in comprehension. In order to facilitate understanding, new activities are introduced using demonstration followed by placing the student through the activity with the additional support of language and or gesture. Placing and gesture are gradually withdrawn until the student is finally able to respond to language alone.

Gross motor skills are therefore utilised to develop personal and spatial awareness, memory and receptive language. It is important to realise also that the physical effects of the activities make an important contribution to the students' welfare. A patient, for example, who after involvement in the programme shows less clumsiness by moving from place to place without personal mishap, is a much more assured and contented individual. He is also less dependent on care staff for treatment to cuts and bruises which were a feature of his more cumbersome past.

Although not all the severely mentally handicapped are capable of developing a social sense, an important feature of the programme is the attempt to develop co-operation with others. Pair, group and class activities can be organised to facilitate this aim. The ability to throw and catch in pairs presents few difficulties for the average adult. For many mentally handicapped the task is tremendously difficult. They have, for instance, to be aware that the partner is ready to receive the ball, that they are sufficiently near to the receiver for the pass to reach him, that the pass is weighted sufficiently carefully for the receiver to be able to catch it, that having made the pass they themselves are prepared to receive the ball back. For the activity to be carried out with overall success, there has to be sufficient awareness not only of self, but also of ones 'partner's' position and relative competence. The development of this awareness seems crucial to the development of co-operation.

From the basic movement of passing balls in pairs a progressive programme of activities has been developed which increases the level of co-operation students are capable of; for example, the challenge might be to make a specified number of passes without dropping the ball, or at a higher level, bringing in a degree of competition by matching pair against pair (or pairs): the objective being to be the first pair to make a specified number of passes. The concept of counting at an elementary level is facilitated by such activities.

The number of activities is limitless. Skill, however, is essential in organising them into a hierarchical progressive system which is designed to meet specific objectives. The perceptuo-motor programmme is not rigid. It is forever changing as staff, through observation of the effects of the programme on students, become more aware of the problems they have, and their own lack of skill in dealing with them. Staff have always been convinced that the programme provides stimulation and enjoyment whilst enhancing personal development for a large number of mentally handicapped students who have the additional major problem of severe behavioural disturbance.

Teaching staff are also additionally involved with those students attending the perceptuo-motor activities in promoting strategies which further develop primary communication skills.

A teacher is allocated five mornings a week to the severely mentally handicapped groups for this purpose. In many ways the behavioural problems of the students are more evident in the rooms allocated for promoting this work than they are in the gymnasium. Students are frequently given to anti-social and dangerous behaviour. It is not an easy matter to determine the roots of such behaviour. Relatively few severely mentally handicapped adults display such gross disturbance. Nevertheless experience at Rampton Hospital has shown that where staff are concerned to involve themselves positively with patients, behaviour problems are greatly reduced.

Two factors appear to be most significant in this process of modifying adverse behaviour. The first is related to the increased attention which the severely mentally handicapped student receives during his pro-gramme. When left to his or her own devices the student has little social contact and consequently his social awareness is considerably stunted.

It would appear that this starvation of a basic need inhibits the overall development of the organism and leaves the individual in a state where he is barely tolerated as a human being. Warm and consistent attention by disciplines at Rampton seems to have assisted a large number of severely mentally handicapped to accommodate more adequately to what appears to them to be a hostile and threatening world.

Attention by itself would not however appear to be a sufficient factor in itself to account for the improvement in the behaviour of severely mentally handicapped patients at Rampton Hospital. As the description of the perceptuo-motor programme above indicates, it is the QUALITY OF THE ATTENTION WHICH IS CRUCIAL. This quality is related to the second factor which appears to be most crucial in assisting the severely mentally handicapped to accommodate to their environment, that is the involvement in purposeful activity.

The lecturer responsible for educational work with the group of students mentioned above works with his nursing colleagues to develop skills and knowledge which will enable students to reach a higher level of social competence than would be possible without skilled intervention. This is the main aim, but as has been discussed, there is a tremendous observable bonus in that the work has reduced the level of adverse behaviour.

In general, as with the basic education programme, the approach is to identify needs through an assessment process. Once established, the meeting of these needs is done through the formulation of specific objectives for each individual patient. Areas of need covered in this particular area are fine motor skills, communications (both speech and manual methods), spatial awareness and number awareness. The range of activities for each area is extensive and important items can be structured progressively facilitating an easy step by step approach to learning.

A similar programme aimed at developing primary communication skills has been implemented with a group of chronically mentally ill students. Teacher involvement with this group amounts to four mornings and four afternoon sessions. Where possible, as is implied by the following description, teachers develop communication skills to as high a level as is possible.

The media by which teachers attempt to restore a more normal personality are art, music, physical education and movement, and handicrafts. Additionally, where patients are demonstrating good progress, teachers reintroduce them to basic skills which are fundamental to social competence.

General (and Academic) Education

In colleges of further education, such areas as basic education would be included in the general education provision. At Rampton Hospital basic education is so crucial to the development or redevelopment of social competency, that it merits a classification of its own. With one exception general education at Rampton is used to identify day-time classroom activities which do not appear to have the development of social competence as their main objective. The exception is part of the domestic science programme.

The domestic science provision has three programmes. The first concerns itself with basic cookery, laundering and hygiene skills, and as it is specific to coping in a flat or self-care hostel is very much connected with the development of social competence. In the second programme the content is more traditional, based as it is on cake and pastry making and preparation of meals requiring more than basic skill. The third programme is concerned with teaching basic cookery skills for the catering industry and might be considered vocational rather than general education provision.

There are two classes involved in the first programme – 'basic household skills'. Each class consists of seven MALE students and meets weekly on Thursday mornings and afternoons respectively. Students are drawn from the villa wards (Chapter II). The programme normally lasts for one term. The tasks to be taught/skills to be acquired are set out on an assessment chart. As each student progresses through the course he is assessed continuously and his chart amended accordingly. At the end of the course the student's profile which has been compiled on the chart is used as a basis for a report to the student's responsible medical officer (R.M.O.) and charge nurse. If insufficient progress has been made, the student will be required to attend the next course. In some cases where students have been on a villa ward for some years they will be asked to repeat the programme.

The programme consists of five areas: preparation of food and table setting, cooking, cleanliness (a. personal, b. household) care and safety, and economy. Each area has five items of skill or knowledge. The items for cooking are (a) Prepares satisfactorily a pot or cup of instant coffee or tea, (b) Prepares for himself a simple hot snack using convenience foods, (c) Can fry eggs, bacon and sausage, (d) Can prepare a full breakfast, (e) Can cook a two course meal.

This example demonstrates that emphasis is placed on the ability of the individual to attend to essential everyday needs.

71

All students eat the food they prepare in lieu of meals they would have on the wards. The social setting of the meal in the classroom provides an opportunity for teachers to enhance and reinforce the social education of students. Particularly is this so, as when frequently happens, guests from the staff are invited to a meal.

The second programme is much more open ended, having no firm and fast aims other than to teach skill in baking and cooking. Three classes meet once a week. Each class consists of seven women students. When meals are cooked students stay longer to eat what they have prepared.

The third programme, basic cookery for the catering industry, was introduced into the programme in response to the needs of patients employed in the patients' kitchen. Hospital cooks in this department observed that many patients had the ability and interest to train as qualified cooks. It was not possible to combine formal training and the main aim, that of the provision of patients' meals, in the normal daily programme of the kitchen. It was agreed that instruction for Part I of the City and Guilds 147 Course – Basic Cookery for the Catering Industry should be undertaken by the education department. Between 1981 and 1983 the course was conducted successfully in the department's education department. Unfortunately City and Guilds then withdrew certification of Part I of the course. The problem of certification was resolved by the West Nottinghamshire College of Further Education who agreed to assess students' work and validate the course. Currently students successfully completing the department's course by the validation of the West Nottinghamshire College are in a position on discharge to take the two year City and Guilds with a remission of one year. Consequently they are in the same position as their predecessors who completed Part I City and Guilds.

The course consists of two, two-and-a-half hour periods a week. It is essentially practical, but some knowledge of theory is required. A further class meets once a week. This class is mainly for students awaiting placement on the main course.

The Associated Examining Board has recently introduced basic tests in a number of subject areas. The department has welcomed the development of these tests and has introduced three courses providing opportunity for students to be examined on their content. The content of two of the courses is very much concerned with skills associated with social competence: these are Health and Hygiene, and Life and Social Skills. However, while the department's aim is to facilitate social competence through these courses, the additional factor that they are examinable places them in the same category as other examination courses. The third A.E.B. basic tests course is Geography.

The two main academic subjects so far provided as classes in the area of general education are mathematics and English.

There are two mathematics classes. While it is considered all students have the potential to attempt at least one of the examinations on offer, there is a wide degree of ability. Concurrently the teacher has to provide for students studying for R.S.A. arithmetic examinations, C.S.E. basic numeracy tests, and Associated Examining Board 'O' and 'A' levels.

The English class also contains a wide range of ability. Students follow work directed at passing A.E.B. basic English, R.S.A. English language and A.E.B. English 'O' level. English syllabuses are increasingly including oral work in their structure, and this is seen by teaching staff to be a welcome and important development.

OTHER ACADEMIC COURSES are available through correspondence courses. There has never been a realistic demand by sufficient students to warrant the formation of academic classes other than for English and mathematics. A number of students have studied individually Russian, French, history, computer studies, economics, geography. Time and facilities are made available for students on correspondence courses in the department during the day. Where it has been evident that the student requires specialist tutorials on their subject, arrangements have been made to bring in specialist staff from outside.

Six students have enrolled on OPEN UNIVERSITY COURSES since the formation of that institution. No one student has completed his degree in the hospital but ALL have passed the subjects they studied thus gaining the necessary credits.

Leisure and Recreational Activities

This provision is relatively extensive. During day-time sessions it is in general restricted to activities organised by the department's physical education section. Classes in recreational physical fitness and games are organised for patients attending occupation department workshops. A recent development has been to organise two sessions a week for those recently admitted into the hospital and who are attending the initial assessment unit. Observations of patients taking part in physical education activities has provided important information for the assessment procedure.

There is considerable pressure on the department for space in the gymnasium during the day time. Currently it is not possible to accommodate all who wish to use it.

The evening school provision has always proved popular and is well supported. It is in competition with other recreational activities, and in order that there are no major clashes of interests, which would not be in the interests of patients, most classes are organised on Monday and Tuesday evenings. Classes include general physical fitness, weight training, badminton, basketball, athletics (summer), astronomy, church music, brass (band) music, guitar, art (three classes), collecting as a hobby, cane work, photography, computer literacy, horticulture and creative writing.

Perhaps the most innovative development in the area of leisure and recreational activities has been the introduction of the Summer School which was first held in 1985.

It was considered a Summer School would meet two basic needs. Firstly it would extend the educational year in the hospital. Secondly it would provide a further opportunity to lessen the regularised pattern of institutional life. If this process could be taken further, the change could be so significant as to provide the opportunity for students to take a holiday.

The educational year at Rampton Hospital is longer than in further education colleges, being forty-three weeks in the year. The first Summer School lasted one week and reduced the Summer break from three to two weeks thus extending the educational year to forty-four weeks.

A feature of the basic educational provision is that its structure has been entirely organised by teachers for students. Students may have a say in the planning of their weekly work, but they have had little say in what should be included in the total structure. The Summer School offered an opportunity for students to be consulted regarding the content of the week's programme. Requests were made to all students to state their preferences for subjects. Ninety returns showed that fifty-five subjects had been suggested. The main demand was for four subjects: soccer coaching, music, art and computer studies.

The subjects chosen for the school were therefore based on suggestions made by prospective students. Another point was the agreement made with nursing and catering staff to have the mid-day meal in the recreation hall adjacent to the education department and recreation area. This arrangement not only made it unnecessary for patients to trek back and forth to their wards at lunch-time but presented a valuable opportunity for staff and students to relate and socialise over a meal. The appreciation of students of these catering and social arrangements was overwhelming.

A programme was formalised consisting of four one-and-a-half hour sessions a day. Each student was to study his main subject for three of the four sessions; on the fourth session he would take part in one of the other three subjects.

Patients were invited to enrol for the Summer School.

Seventy-two applications were received of which fifty-eight were accepted.

An evaluation of the Summer School is included in Chapter V.

The Teaching Staff – Complement

Details of the exact full-time complement of staff has been given in Chapter II.

The Teaching Staff – Background

Full Time Staff

It is difficult to summarise the previous background experience of the teaching staff at Rampton Hospital. Nevertheless, despite the wide differences, two groupings have tended to emerge.

Teachers either started their professional careers in infant or primary education with a general approach to education or they were specialist subject teachers in secondary education having little experience of a general approach. Both groupings however have significant contributions to make to the curriculum in a special hospital. The generalists, because of their experience in teaching basic educational skills to a wide range of abilities, have the expertise to organise individualised and small group learning and the knowledge and awareness of appropriate learning strategies in basic education. The subject specialists, in addition to the value of their subject to the curriculum, have usually been involved in working part-time in adult further education and youth work. Their experience in teaching adults and adolescents has proved invaluable in modifying the child-centred approach in teaching basic educational skills which their generalist teaching colleagues have training in. The combination of experience of the two groups has made it possible to develop basic educational work for patients which is appropriate to both their status as adults/adolescents and their ability.

75

Currently (1987) there are fourteen full-time teaching staff in employment, with a further appointment to be made in September.

Part Time Teaching Staff

Sessional staff are used extensively at Rampton Hospital. Part of the sessional teaching is covered by full-time staff working additional hours. However most work of this nature is carried out by a further nineteen to twenty part-time staff. The large majority of these staff are employed full-time by the hospital in other capacities. They have specialist qualifications and have attended part-time teacher training in adult and/or further education.

This pool of talent available to the education department from other disciplines has proved of inestimable value. It includes those of other disciplines who are highly motivated and dedicated to their work. Additionally their position in other disciplines has frequently opened up resources for education which would not normally be available. That they have keys and are free to move about the hospital is a not inconsiderable factor to be taken into consideration in planning classes.

Support Staff

Of the English special hospitals, Rampton is the only education department directly employing clerical/typing assistance. Twenty hours weekly are allocated for this duty. It is significant that since the post was established in 1976, both typists have become interested in teaching and have completed their City and Guilds Teaching Certificate. Subsequently they have both taught typing in the education programme.

A recent establishment has been the post of part-time audio-visual technician in the patients' further education department. This has proved necessary for the maintenance and monitoring of the increasing range of audio-visual aids and computers, and to assist in the development of teaching aids: worksheets and other materials used in teaching.

The Teaching Staff – Professional Development

The complex nature of the task facing teachers at Rampton is such that careful consideration has to be given to the development of personal knowledge and skill. A lack of recognition of this requirement would result in a stagnation of ideas and a curriculum which had little in common with the aims of the hospital or the needs of students.

In-service training within the department has to take into account two areas of responsibility. Firstly, it has to ensure that staff have the knowledge and skill to cope directly with their work within departmental boundaries i.e. intra-departmental. Secondly, there is an additional requirement which would not appear to be so much in evidence in main stream education, and that is an understanding of the roles of other disciplines within the overall organisation. This is essential if the problem of meeting patients' needs is to proceed along multidisciplinary lines. There is therefore a requirement to consider and ultimately implement inter-departmental in-service training.

Intra-departmental in-service training has three components. The first component has proved to be the most significant. It is based on a weekly curriculum development meeting which is obligatory for full-time staff and to which part-time staff have an open invitation. Basically the meeting is concerned with problem solving related to curriculum development or the development of knowledge and skill. Currently, for example, the Basic Education, level III, (Basic Studies Course) is in the process of a full revision. The process has been lengthy, lasting for over a year. Though time consuming, all staff have been involved in the processes of curriculum development: identifying, researching and reviewing relevant issues, formulating objectives and assessment items, deciding on hierarchies, organising material and so on. The project has involved discussions, reading and planning of curriculum issues. Through the total process staff have gained a deeper knowledge of their work and the tools they require in developing their teaching strategies.

Major projects like the review of the Basic Education level III (Basic Studies) programme are not unending features of the curriculum meetings. They are frequently interspersed by much shorter topics. For example, staff may present a case-study of a student who is giving rise for concern (or conversely has shown great facility in his studies) or present a paper on a topic of significance, i.e. one which would appear to offer something to an aspect of the department's educational provision. The paper may be based on an article, or lecture, or the contents of a course. Whatever it is, the member of staff making the presentation is concerned with spreading the information to a wider but involved audience.

The second component is traditional to the main-stream education service. Teaching staff are given every encouragement to attend short courses organised by a number of outside bodies. Continuous refreshment of ideas and knowledge are particularly important to staff in

77

special hospitals because of the inherent isolation from mainstream education.

The third level of intra-departmental training for in service education is annual secondment. This topic was described earlier in the chapter on Context when discussing the independence of the education department. It is of particular importance, both for the widening and deepening of the range of professional expertise and knowledge available to the department and equally for the opportunity it provides staff for personal development.

Interdisciplinary in contrast to intra-disciplinary in-service training exists, but because of the immense problems which are apparent in organising and focussing on issues affecting the co-operative strategy of a number of disciplines, there is as yet no level of development equivalent to that of the education department's first component in training, i.e. training on the job. Almost all the training at interdisciplinary level consists of courses either within or outside the hospital and which are attended by more than one hospital discipline.

Within the hospital it is mandatory for all staff to attend an induction course on appointment to the hospital. This course lasts for three days for all staff except nursing, who continue for three weeks. Another mandatory course is the health, safety and fire study day which staff attend once a year. All nursing and occupations staff attend a restraints course which lasts two weeks. Four teaching staff have attended this course and it is intended that eventually all education personnel will be trained in this aspect.

The staff education centre in the hospital is mainly concerned with nurse training. It does, however, arrange courses for the hospital staff. Teaching staff have attended for counselling, psycho-therapy, behaviour modification and other related subjects. Additionally teaching staff have assisted with the running of courses in the staff education department. These have been concerned with drama, music and art, and occasionally the work of teachers in the education of the mentally disordered.

Currently the senior education officer, patients' education department, is a member of the curriculum development team for the mental handicap nursing course and advances in mental handicap policies.

The short courses held in the staff education centre are frequently followed up by teachers in attendance, who, with colleagues from other disciplines, enrol in outside courses which examine subjects like psychotherapy in greater depth. The experience and knowledge of the teachers are then passed on to other staff in the in-service curriculum meeting.

Currently within the education department there appears to be a greater awareness of and sensitivity to those factors affecting patients' behaviour which are traditionally the prerogative of other disciplines to understand and treat. This heightened perception enables teachers to be more skilled in listening to their students' general problems, but with a recognition that any interventive action on their part requires the agreement and co-operation of other disciplines. The additional skill of the teaching staff has been acquired through the inter-departmental in-service training process.

The main strength of the department's in-service training strategy is that it enables all full-time staff to be capable of making a significant contribution to the basic education programme. This programme, in terms of need, is the most important in the curriculum; it is also the largest in relation to allocation of teaching time and resources. As it is seen as the core component, it has always followed that staff must have the necessary training to be able to take or assist with a group of students.

It is evident that a teacher in a special hospital must be well trained with a commitment to the further development of his skills and knowledge. Teaching staff must also be adaptable. They have, for example, to accept a situation whereby, unlike in schools and colleges, they are not the dominant profession. Consequently in their preparation, teaching and assessment it is obligatory that they take account of variables which in their normal environment they would not have to consider. They must also adjust to a situation, whereby although their work facilitates the expressed aims of the hospital, they will run counter to the opinion of a powerful lobby which believes that a special hospital is solely a place of containment, and that rehabilitation only starts on discharge or transfer of a patient.

In summary, observation and experience leads to a conclusion that teachers in special hospitals require personal qualities of tolerance, tenacity, resilience and a good sense of humour. They must be capable of empathy with their students and meaningful co-operation with other disciplines. Their job satisfaction, like that of members of other professional disciplines, depends on their ability to cope with the exacting nature of their duties. That the majority of teachers have survived and gained reward from their work is a tribute to their forward-looking attitudes and well balanced personalities.

Most of the discussion on staff development refers mainly to full-time teachers. Many part-time staff involve themselves in in-service training. Unfortunately their conditions of service and the lack of formal financial support are major disincentives to a higher level of commitment. Nevertheless recent major developments in l.e.a. provision for in-service training should, in the future, ensure a better deal for part-time staff.

Resources

The buildings allocated to the education department were listed in Chapter II. Each of the seven classrooms in that list is well resourced. Perhaps the most significant feature in each room is a B.B.C. Computer, complete with a full range of accessories and a wide range of software. As all rooms are used at some time for basic education, there is also a language master and a tape recorder. The relevant books and teaching materials on classroom shelves are wide in range and in sufficient supply. Patients are not allowed the use of money in the hospital. A problem arises when considering skills needed by the patient when he leaves the hospital: one of these skills is the use of money. The education department therefore holds a float of real money which is used in teaching or assisting students to reacquire money skills. Additionally the department has been able to provide students with the opportunity to familiarise themselves with the telephone by the provision of special resources.

Teachers also have the use of video equipment – both feed-back and recording, including the use of a camera. These items with slide, tape, and film projectors are available from the technician. Also backing up the books and teaching materials in the classroom is a central resource area offering a wide variety of choice. Perhaps the main compensation for teachers involved in the most difficult task of remedial/basic education in a special hospital is their recourse to excellent facilities.

The domestic science room is equally well resourced. It has four stations, each containing a sink and two cookers. Additionally there is a washing machine, tumble dryer, refrigerator, freezer, and micro-wave oven.

The gymnasium has sufficient resources and space to accommodate most major and minor indoor games, gymnastics, fitness and weight training, and trampolining. In summer extensive sports field facilities are available immediately adjacent to the gymnasium.

Teaching Methods

It can be appreciated that teaching methods must attempt to fit a wide variety of circumstances. In the area of basic education students are placed in small groups containing six to eight students. The main teaching method in these groups is individualised teaching. Each student has a work programme based on planned objectives. The objectives have been defined to meet those personal needs which have been highlighted through the initial education assessment process. Individual students therefore work at their own particular level on subject matter which at the time is most appropriate to their needs.

The teacher moves around the group giving her attention to one individual at a time. It is extremely important in structuring individualised teaching that the teacher has resources which help her to cope with the very demanding situation of dealing with six to eight different educational programmes at one and the same time. Where nurses are involved in assisting teachers in the basic education programme, there is a considerable boost to efficiency and morale.

Though individualised teaching remains the most dominant method in basic education groups, it is not used exclusively. It has been found that a number of money and time skills can be taught and reinforced with students working together in small groups. Additionally group work is appropriate for role-play and socio drama, watching films and other animated visual displays.

Individual teaching in contrast to individualised teaching is extremely expensive in resources. It is necessary to consider its use at Rampton Hospital in some cases. Certain students require assistance with basic skills without the distraction of others around them. Others, it is felt, require sex education without the possible embarrassment of others being present. Assistance with speech and conversation are initially best served on a one to one basis. Some students are in a 'class of their own' in certain academic subjects and it is necessary to arrange specialised individual assistance in order that their studies can progress. This is most readily done by correspondence course, but occasionally it is necessary to arrange tutorials with specialised staff in the department.

The mathematics and English examination classes, although containing able students, have responded to an organisation based on a mixture of teaching methods. The individualised approach is used to cope with the apparent wide differences in attainment shown in a group of individuals who might possibly be considered to be of similar ability. Group work is used where it seems feasible for students to study together on material which is suitable for them all. The class teacher of both subjects, nevertheless, sets aside part of the time available to lead the whole class in an aspect of the curriculum which he feels is beneficial for all his students.

Whichever teaching approach is appropriate, there appear to be basically three learning styles in operation. This is apparent in all the classroom activities.

Perhaps the most obvious style, considering that learning and teaching take place within defined parameters, is that of TEACHER DIRECTED LEARNING. This approach might not be acceptable to some adult educators, as they see the initiative and motivation for real learning arising only from within the student. Nevertheless a starting point for many of the students is a realisation that here is someone – the teacher – who is aware of many of his problems and is willing to assist. It should be realised that many students in the early stages lack the mental effort and will to initiate their own learning or to want to have a say in what they should learn. Without the external force and drive of the teacher in the early days of attendance very few students would progress with their studies.

Nevertheless teachers are not wholly content to continue with a teacher directed style of learning. It is a less arduous task for themselves and certainly more beneficial to the student when organisation of work to be done is a partnership. A more INTERACTIVE STYLE OF LEARNING is therefore apparent with many students who have become self motivated. This is most obvious in planning the work to be done in each week by students on the basic education course. The student selects the topics he wants to cover, in consultation with the teacher. The teacher then assists in planning suitable and appropriate resources which will facilitate learning in the area of the student's choice.

A minority of students use a third style of learning – THE SELF-DIRECTED STYLE. This is most obvious with students of above average ability and/or who have a distinct and driving passion to master an area of knowledge or skill. The education department's main role for such students is to facilitate their learning through counselling and the provision of resources. For example, a student on basic education level III became interested in computer programming during the time he was using the computer to assist with his spelling problem. He taught himself to programme through his own efforts to a very competent standard. Another student became fluent in Russian. The progress of both these students is set out in the chapter on evaluation (pp 127-129).

There are therefore three main learning styles in operation in the patients' further education department at Rampton: (1) teacher directed, (2) interactive, (3) self or student directed. Obviously these styles are not mutually exclusive and most learning takes place using a mixture of approaches.

Summary

The structure of the curriculum of the patients' further education department at Rampton Hospital is based on meeting the very wide and diverse needs of its students. Most effort and resources are allocated to the development of adequate levels of basic education. This is so, as it is recognised that the ability to survive in the open community depends on the development of a functional level of social competence. The education department's programme of basic education and life and social skills is an integral part of the hospital's policy to prepare patients for life in the open community. The complexity of the task of developing adequate levels of basic education is reflected in the need to structure three levels of provision and to meet individual needs through individual programmes and individualised teaching methods.

A recognition of the need to intensify effort in the preparation of a patient for the outside world at the time prior to discharge has been met by the establishment of a vocational preparation unit. The education department is involved with nurse and occupation disciplines in identifying and remediating those deficiencies which are seen as priorities in the weeks before the patient leaves the hospital.

The needs of the severely and profoundly mentally handicapped and the chronically mentally ill are met in two ways, both in close co-ordination and co-operation with nursing staff. A programme of perceptuo-motor activities is implemented in the gymnasium. Additionally a teacher assists in the development of receptive and expressive spoken communication skills, in manual forms of communication (e.g. MAKATON), visual and auditory discrimination and fine motor skill development.

A general and academic provision is available. Most students are encouraged at some time in their stay to attend basic cookery classes. Academic study is provided from basic R.S.A. arithmetic and English examinations to Open University courses.

Academic study and the availability of leisure and recreational classes provide opportunity for personal development, and extend the range of activities on offer to patients. The widening and extension of opportunity is particularly valuable, as closed institutions by their structure are considerably restricted in their ability to provide a wide range of social activities for their inmates.

Fourteen full-time, supplemented by a greater number of part-time staff and supported by a technician and clerical officer make up the staffing complement which directs and implements the curriculum. Teaching staff are well trained and make available to the department a wide area of specialisms.

A major source of compensation to teachers in their difficult task is the availability of good resources in sufficient supply to meet most requirements.

Teaching methods used in the curriculum vary according to circumstances. Major emphasis is placed on individualised teaching, but individual, group and class methods are also used. Three learning styles are apparent, either in use singly or in combination. These are teacher-directed, interactive and self (or student) – directed learning.

Chapter V

EVALUATION

"We think that money spent on expanding the educational facilities at Rampton would certainly be money well spent."

(Boynton, J., 1980: 98)

This comment from the Boynton Report was based on the opinions of the members who made up the Rampton Hospital Management Review Team (Boynton Committee) and their educational assessor, Mr. C. A. Norman, formerly Her Majesty's Inspector (Staff Inspector at the Department of Education and Science) (Boynton, J., 1980: 96). It is a valuable comment in that it represents the views of an independent group of highly qualified and experienced esteemed individuals as to the worth of education in Rampton Special Hospital. From their observations one can assume that in general the education department was carrying out its tasks in a satisfactory manner. It is therefore an evaluative statement. The following account will attempt to provide a basis to the opinion expressed by the Boynton Committee.

The main tasks of the education department were set out above in Chapter III, i.e. personal development and the development of social competence. These tasks cannot be fulfilled, however, unless the department has made sufficient development in organisation and resources. The department has a primary role in providing the patient with the same kind of educational opportunities that would be open to him in the outside community. In meeting this role an attempt has been made to establish a further education department within the hospital. The evaluation of the education department at Rampton Hospital will therefore be presented in three parts: the development of an educational service, the development of social competence, and of personal development.

Educational Research

Attempts to research those areas of educational provision selected for evaluation in this study of the Rampton Hospital education department are not unique to the field of educational research. They are but several aspects of a wider spectrum of research which attempts to establish the meaning, nature, management/organisation and effectiveness of education. Consequently education research is specialised and multi-faceted, involving practitioners from the fields of philosophy, history, management, sociology, psychology and the curriculum.

Whatever subject forms the basis of the research, one of two main approaches will normally be used in carrying out a process of evaluation. These are known as the 'orthodox', scientific or quantitative approach on the one hand and the qualitative approach on the other. Normally the nature of the subject of research determines the selection of the research approach, but adherents of either approach often see 'their' way as being exclusively valid and reliable.

The quantitative approach tests stated hypotheses. It is concerned with the organisation and management of research methods and statistical techniques which enable the researcher to reach a conclusion on that which he has stated as a hypothesis.

In the following evaluation of the development of social competence at Rampton, that part which concerns itself with the comparison of differences in educational attainment in basic education, before and after tuition, is an incomplete example of a quantitative approach in educational research. Although all research instruments in use are reliable and valid, and statistical methods applied are appropriate, the total project as research is incomplete because of a failure to sufficiently control external variables which could have a bearing on results. That is, although the average student on a basic education course makes significant progress, this cannot be attributed solely to educational intervention. It cannot be ruled out that other factors or forces in the hospital may have made a contribution to the improvement.

This qualification apart, the statistical information for the basic education levels I and II course, because it covers a significant period of ten years, has an inherent strength which could be seen to outweigh the problem of controlling research variables by such contrived methods as control groups. The strength lies in the fact that for ten consecutive years (apart for one year) results show a consistent level of progress. Progress has been achieved at the same time as external variables, which could have contributed to the improvement, have changed. The variable which has been most consistent in the period – educational provision – can be claimed, therefore, to have made the major significant contribution to the increase in skill and knowledge in the basic education levels I and II courses.

Information related to students' progress, collected and analysed over ten years, could under the circumstances put forward, be acceptable in rejecting a null hypothesis that educational provision would not improve basic education skills. Consequently in the following evaluation of the development of social competence, that section which examines basic education I and II could claim to meet the rigours of a quantitative research approach. This is important, for additional validity is, as a result, provided to the evaluation. A more substantial claim can be made therefore for student progress to be the sole result of educational provision.

The strategies used in the following evaluation at Rampton would be, in the main, more closely associated with the second of the two proposed main educational research approaches, namely the qualitative. There are several methods associated with this approach, details of which are outlined in a seminal paper on research in adult education by M. Pilsworth and R. Ruddock (Pilsworth, M. and Ruddock, R., 1975).

These research methods claim to illuminate understanding and perception of education. The biographical accounts in this evaluation illustrate how a number of students have been helped considerably in developing social competence and personal maturity. They are crucial to an understanding and perception of education's effect from the point of view of the individual. Although the presentation may not be fully acceptable as a biographical analysis research method it has relied on the main principles of the method in its overall form.

One of the most significant features of education in Rampton Hospital has been its development. The evaluation of this development forms the first of the three aspects of the education department to be examined in the following account. Although descriptive, the nature of the account attempts to follow sound research principles. In so doing it not only states what has occurred in the development of education but attempts to answer why and how changes in a number of areas have come about. The evaluation is linked to methods normally employed in historical and sociological research.

In carrying out an evaluation of the patients' further education department at Rampton Hospital every effort has been made to ensure that the process has been based on authentic educational research methods.

The Development of an Educational Service

The development of an educational service within a closed institution would appear to be more crucial to the lives of patients than the external community provision is to the general population. Few patients before admission to the hospital have ever attended further, adult or higher education. This position is markedly reversed within the hospital, with approximately three fifths of the patient population taking part in some form of education. It is accepted that a significant percentage of this attendance arises through the encouragement of patients by treatment disciplines to attend classes. Nevertheless there is a substantial number of patients who normally on the outside would never consider attendance at college or centre, yet in Rampton Hospital are keen to be members of a wide variety of courses.

Primarily it has to be recognised that all inmates of closed institutions are separated totally from their previous cultural background. In their own neighbourhood they neglected or ignored educational provision because there were more attractive alternatives. These alternatives are no longer available in Rampton as a special hospital, so much so that life is restricted to the ward or the work area with weekly visits to the recreational hall for bingo and Saturday dance and social and the occasional concert or cinema. Church also provides opportunity for a change in environment and spiritual refreshment. Although these visits are welcome, they lack the spontaneous freedom which is attached to similar outings outside. Education provides an additional area to those noted previously, where patients are provided with the opportunity to give more diversity to their lives. It does not in general overcome the problem of a lack of spontaneity of choice. However education appears relatively more attractive than it was on the outside.

This observation coincides with Goffman's (Goffman, E., 1961: 67) view that in any closed institution inmates will try to make life as bearable as possible by attempting to escape from the ever present close control of the system. Education is therefore a very important medium in this process, providing involvement for patients in a wide range of academic, social and practical activities.

The education department has developed partly in response to what patients want, and also to what treatment disciplines see as necessary.

(a) *Buildings*

In 1969 the education department inherited two classrooms, a domestic science room and a new gymnasium. These resources were inadequate, and while the three classrooms then under construction were completed classes were held in the visiting room.

During 1970 the department moved into the three new classrooms. These were small and inadequate and could not accommodate the educational programme. They had been designed to accommodate the education department as it stood before it was taken over by the l.e.a. The gymnasium was a valuable resource but the domestic science room and the original two classrooms were on three separate sites, making the provision of a co-ordinated daily programme difficult.

Some eighteen months later the department took over a building which had previously housed the weaving shed. The two satellite classrooms and the domestic science room were handed over to the occupations department in exchange for this building. The vacated 'new' classrooms were converted into a library.

The acquired building was not structurally modified to any great extent – except that one part was converted into a domestic science room. In addition, a large area provided four teaching areas which were left open-plan, and a room provided a fifth teaching area.

In 1979/80 two additional teaching areas, two offices and a staffroom were added to the education department. Additional work was carried out in 1984/85 to the 'open plan' area converting it into four self-contained classrooms.

An agreement some three years ago by all parties concerned resulted in an exchange of the buildings housing the hospital church and gymnasium. The current gymnasium for which the education department is responsible is well equipped and large enough to accommodate two double and one single badminton courts.

Over the past seventeen years there has been substantial development in meeting the needs of the education department for adequate buildings. Additionally, as has been mentioned earlier, staff work in buildings which are not the direct responsibility of the senior education officer, e.g. wards, vocational preparation unit and activity areas.

(b) *Staffing*
Full-time Staff
Table 3 Full-time Staffing.

Year	HDII	SL	LII	LI	AssL	AssocL	A/V Technician	Total	Approx Patient Population
1969	–	–	–	2*	1	–	–	3	1100
1974			1	5*	1	–	–	7	1100
1977	1	–	1	7	–	–	–	9	1000
1981	1		2†	9	–	–	–	12	800
1987	1	1	4	8	–	1	1	16	550

* One LI held a special responsibility allowance
† One LII was designated deputy senior education officer

Table 3 shows that there has been a significant increase in the full-time staffing of the education department over the years since the opening date in 1969. This is more notable when taken in relationship with the patient population. The ratio of teaching staff to patients in 1969 was 1:366; in 1987 1:37.

Career development opportunities have also improved within the department. In 1969 the Senior Education Officer (S.E.O.) was a Lecturer Grade I with a special responsibility allowance. Since 1975 the S.E.O. has been on a Head of Department II scale. Currently five additional posts to the S.E.O. are graded above Lecturer I level.

Part-time Staff

Table 4. Part-time Staff 1980-87

Year	No. of staff	Weekly Teaching Hours
80	16	60
81	17	62
82	17	75
83	15	70
84	22	99
85	19	91
86	22	100
87	23	112

Part-time staff have always made a major contribution to the teaching programme at Rampton Hospital. Table 4 shows an increase in part-time staffing both in number of staff and teaching hours available since the Boynton Report was published in 1980.

(c) Development in Organisation

Commensurate with the development of staffing, buildings and resources, there has been a corresponding development in organisation. Though here discussed last in this section on the development of the education department, it is the organisational development which has prompted development in buildings and staffing. The organisational development would appear to have evolved over three major periods of time: 1969-75, 1975-1980 and 1980 to the present.

In 1969 an initial survey in which almost every patient in the hospital was interviewed was carried out in the first month of the department's existence. Results from the survey indicated a high level of literacy and numeracy problems. These results affected organisational development, for during the next five years the department organised its resources and planning in meeting the needs of those students with the most severe problems in these areas. Additionally resources were allocated to developing the perceptuo-motor activity work with the profoundly and severely mentally handicapped group. The S.E.O. was given time to concentrate on essential planning and organisation but at this stage he was teaching for more than half his contractual time.

Evening school continued at a substantial level on Monday and Tuesday evenings. Subjects in this area were mainly in the fields of art, light crafts, music, drama, cookery and physical education (inclusive of games). It was evident that several patients were capable of academic work and assistance in this area was provided mainly through correspondence courses.

The next stage in organisational development was between 1975-1980. In 1975 the department became independent of the Retford Adult Education Centre and full responsibility for all aspects of administration and organisation were transferred to the S.E.O. His line of communication was now established directly with the Further Education Department at County Hall. During the next five years, up to the inquiry carried out by Boynton, emphasis was placed in consolidating the experience gained in teaching students with severe learning problems in communication areas and developing a suitable programme of basic educational skills for students whose literacy and numeracy needs were not so relatively acute. This programme was the basic studies course which was discussed in the previous chapter and whose evaluation will be presented later. There was a marked growth in basic education in the first half of this stage.

Work continued with the severely and profoundly mentally handicapped patient through the perceptuo-motor programmes in the gymnasium. Additionally to this work a teacher had for some years carried out percussion and drama with the students attending the gymnasium programme. A request was made for this teacher to increase his involvement with activity groups for the severely mentally handicapped and chronically mentally ill. This request was to prove significant in that growth of numbers of full-time staff has, from the time of this request, mainly resulted from other disciplines asking for teacher assistance with their treatment programmes.

During this stage there was a reduction in part-time staff and a subsequent loss of evening school classes. Classes were taken off on a Monday evening in order that ward staff could carry out their own activities with patients on the ward. There were a number of factors which made it impossible for this nursing arrangement to be sustained for more than a few months. Subsequently education was requested to arrange new classes. Unfortunately the l.e.a. was in a period of financial restraint and was unwilling to allow money to be spent on additional classes.

Academic education continued at a low level of provision, although examination level classes in English and mathematics were introduced in addition to the correspondence course arrangements.

The current stage of development follows the publication of the Boynton Committee report in 1980. Reference to the tables on staffing (Tables 3 and 4) shows a significant increase in staffing levels and indicates increased organisational development.

A team leader was appointed to both the morning and afternoon basic education groups. The main reasons for these appointments were first to support teaching staff with their difficult tasks, and second to provide cover when teachers were required to attend case conferences. Case reviews of patients have increased markedly in this period and have placed significant demand on teaching resources.

Additionally on two occasions, one of them current, the department has had to make special provisions within the basic education programme for deaf patients. A class now exists for deaf patients and meets every morning.

Basic education was further strengthened by the introduction of new technology, in particular computers and video equipment. Supporting this introduction was the appointment of an audio-visual technician for twenty hours a week.

Academic or subject-based education showed some expansion. An additional examination class for mathematics was introduced. Classes in geography, health and hygiene, life and social skills were set up with the intention of sitting the Associated Examining Board's Basic Attainment Tests.

The 'new' larger gymnasium, with its potential for greater accommodation, was utilised for an expansion of physical education classes in the daytime. These classes were made up of patients attending various occupations workshops. It was considered that physical education would provide a valuable diversionary activity to their normal work programme.

Table 4 shows an increase of the availability of part-time teaching hours. A large proportion of these hours were used to increase the number of evening school classes. The evening school programme is now more extensive than at any other time in the education department's existence.

The trend already noted in the previous stage of the development of organisation, in which demands for staffing came from other disciplines, made significant progress. A member of staff was allocated full-time to the activity groups organised by the nursing service for severely mentally handicapped and chronically mentally ill patients. This member of staff will be supported by a colleague as the most recent appointment takes up his position in the department, thus increasing staffing levels to two in the activity areas.

A teacher is employed full-time in the high-dependency ward for women. This is a most demanding and exacting job. Additionally the Vocational Preparation Unit makes demands on the educational service. One teacher works full-time in the department supported by a second, teaching five half mornings a week.

It is in this post-Boynton stage that the education department has been called on to assist with treatment areas that are normally considered under therapy. Time-tabling, both within and extra-department, reflects a development in art therapy, sex education and counselling and psychotherapy. A further significant organisational development in this stage has been the annual Summer School. This has provided a major break-through in the provision of education to patients in a closed institution.

In the years 1969-1987 the education department at Rampton Hospital has made steady growth. It has continued to expand, though the patient population in the same period has halved. There has been significant progress in the provision of education for those with inadequate skills in literacy and numeracy. The department has become increasingly sensitive to the needs of its students, this being reflected in the wide variety of educational subjects and activities, and therapeutic processes it is involved in.

Perhaps the most striking feature of recent development is teacher involvement, at the request of other disciplines, in areas not under direct control of the education department. One is hopeful that this development signifies an acceptance of the teacher in the total hospital organisational structure.

The Development of Social Competence

Education, like other disciplines in special hospitals, is concerned with the physical (as opposed to medical) treatment of patients. Physical treatment is concerned with the development of social competence as one of its primary areas. Social competence has been described above as a process which assists patients to cope more adequately with the problems of living in an open society. Inherent in this idealised position is that the former special hospital patient in society will conform within the boundaries of social requirements and the law.

This account has described how the education department at Rampton Hospital groups together subjects and areas of education which ostensibly assist patients to acquire skills they need if higher levels of social competence are to be developed or acquired. In attempting an evaluation of the education department's effectiveness in developing social competence one must be aware that although skill and knowledge acquisition in a number of educational areas are necessary to the development of social competence, there is no guarantee that their acquirement will ultimately affect the crucial nature of social competence. That is, the individual may become more competent and skilful without any apparent sign that the development is affecting his awareness and obligations to society.

Where social competence is unaffected as a natural sequence to the development of skills which are normally thought to be vital parts of the total concept, there are obvious dangers. The individual may leave hospital more individually skilful, but his attitude to society totally unaffected. His higher level of individual competence may be utilised to the detriment of society as a whole and purely in the interests of self. This can be seen in relationship to skills taught by the education department.

Within the educational framework it is quite reasonable to assist a patient who is extremely inarticulate or who is extremely anxious when having to converse with others. The development of skills associated with spoken language is a major area of the basic education levels I and II areas. Several of the skills taught are related to the use of telephones. There are a number of excellent reasons why all members of the community should be proficient in the use of private and public telephones. They are a major facility in providing people with the opportunity to talk to friends, thus enhancing their quality of life. For those who have always required help and assistance in conducting their lives, the telephones which connect them with caring agencies and emergency services are vital. Telephones enable citizens, who find themselves in emergencies where it is their social duty to assist in the resolving of the situation, to call on the appropriate emergency services. One cannot be certain that, in teaching mentally disordered patients the uses of telephones, and how to make calls, the positive aims of the process will be achieved. Individual skills may be developed in using phones and in conveying thoughts and messages to appropriate 'subscribers'. Nevertheless the patient in the community may use his skills outside the boundaries of social competence. He may cause considerable disruption to the emergency services by making false calls. There is the possibility that unfriendly or sexually loaded calls be made to strangers. Finally he may choose to ignore his skill when it would be to his advantage to use it in seeking advice and assistance.

The dangers in claiming that certain prescribed areas of activity assist institutions to fulfil their rehabilitative aims have been highlighted by Sean McConville (McConville, 1974: 110, 111). His discussion is in relationship to penal establishments, and hence caution is required in understanding that his comments may not be directly applicable to a special hospital and its patients. Nevertheless there appears to be sufficient similarity between the rehabilitative goals of both prisons and special hospitals for his comments to have some pertinance to the discussion.

McConville argues that in the penal system, medical, psychiatric, educational and vocational disciplines are able to achieve their objectives, but only in relationship to their own individual spheres of work. He accepts that frequently they are very effective in this respect. Nevertheless his qualification is

> "curing syphilis, replacing diseased teeth, adjusting an offender to homosexuality, detoxifying an addict, successes in teaching inmates to read or to pass high school equivalent examinations, or developing journeyman level mechanical skills – these need not either individually or collectively add up to rehabilitation, if by the latter term we imply a pattern of non-criminal behaviour. In fact we could accomplish all of these desirable goals and turn out a more competent, more dangerous, more sophisticated criminal".
>
> (McConville, 1975: 110-111)

In special hospitals a similar picture to that which exists in the penal field is very evident. Psychiatrists, psychologists, social workers, occupation officers, nurses and teachers all claim that they work successfully with patients in teaching skills and adjusting attitudes. Their work is a necessary condition to successful rehabilitation, a concept which is inclusive of social competence. The problem remains, however, that no one individual discipline, or the united workforce of all disciplines i.e. the multi-disciplinary team, can be certain that what they are trying to achieve is sufficient conditions for the attainment of effective rehabilitation.

Part of the case for having education in special hospitals rested on the education department's contribution to the development of social competence. This point of view need not be invalid, because it is unable to quantify its exact contribution to this major factor in the rehabilitation process. Other disciplines involved in treatment are exactly in the same position. Education is still essential because of its contribution in developing skills and knowledge in those areas which are necessary to the development of social competence. It is crucial that there is a continuous evaluation in this aspect of its work, so that skills and areas of knowledge not yet recognised are uncovered and brought into the education programme. Additionally, as a profession committed to change as its raison d'etre, education should be seeking to understand how its work can be sufficient to the development of social competence. From past experience this search for a solution would seem to lie in the ability of teaching staff to establish relationships with students which develop maturity and an understanding of humanity.

It is most obvious that staff of all disciplines have the ability to affect patients' 'moral' development through meaningful and effective inter-personal relationships. However, the extent and degree to which this is successful is almost impossible to quantify. It has been said that the rate of re-admission to special hospitals is less than to penal institutions. This might be used tentatively as an indication of some success, but cannot be seen to be a reliable or valid measure.

How far has the education department been successful in the development of social competence? From the discussion so far it is plain that any attempt to answer this question has to be qualified. What is attempted below is firstly a presentation of statistics for basic education over a number of years, which demonstrate progression in specific communication skills. These are skills which are necessary to the development of social competence but are not of themselves sufficient for its attainment. Secondly, a number of 'pen portraits' provide more personal and individual accounts of the progress made by students.

The Development of Social Competence
(a) *Basic Education Level I and II (Remedial Education)*

The Progress Assessment Chart 2 has been described earlier in discussing the structure of the curriculum (Chapter IV) and as one of the main assessment forms used by the department (Chapter III).

All students assessed on the P.A.C. 2 who are subsequently found to be underdeveloped in communication skills are recommended for basic education level I, attending the department every morning, or level II, making three afternoon attendances weekly.

The initial assessment acts as a baseline in assessing progress in the education department. Each year, on the anniversary of starting classes, students are reassessed on the P.A.C. 2. On second and subsequent reassessments, although note is made of progress from the previous year, most emphasis is placed on the difference between initial and current assessments.

Tables 5, 6a, b and c show that records have been kept since 1975 of initial and annual reassessments of students attending basic education levels I and II. The average time elapsing between initial assessment and reassessment (columns b and c of Tables 6a, 6b and 6c) is identical to the mean time of students on the course (Table 5). For example, for the twenty-five students of borderline handicap in 1979 the mean time between initial assessment and reassessment was twenty-two months.

Comparison between the number of students attending the course (Table 2, Chapter IV) and those being reassessed (Table 5) shows that between less than a half and three quarters are retested. There are three reasons why a more satisfactory figure is not achieved. First, records between 1980 and 1985 indicate that ten per cent of students have special needs requiring programmes differing from those itemised by the P.A.C.2. These include deaf, mentally ill with symptoms of thought disorder still extant and severely mentally handicapped patients. Second, a large number of students leave classes before the date of reassessment through transfer or discharge from the hospital. Finally, although not a major problem, some students withdraw from classes for personal reasons.

A more complete evaluation of levels I and II of basic education would be possible if all students allocated educational placements were able to be reassessed. Nevertheless there is reason to believe that those who are retested are representative of the total student number.

Evaluation of basic education I and II is possible by two means. First an external validation is available using the Progress Evaluation Index (P.E.I.) (Gunzburg, H., undated). Second the 't' test has been used to assess the significance of the mean improvement between initial assessment and retesting over the ten years 1975 and 1977 to 1985 inclusive.

Gunzburg (Gunzburg, H., 1968: 96) states that the P.E.I. measures the level of achievement, comparing it with the average attainment of those with similar intellectual functioning. The standards or norms Gunzburg sets out in the P.E.I. are arranged under three broad ranges of intellectual functioning as: moderate mental handicap (W.A.I.S. I.Q. 40 to 54), mild mental handicap (W.A.I.S. I.Q. 55 to 69) and borderline mental handicap (W.A.I.S. I.Q. 70 to 84). The results obtained from students on basic education I and II are presented under these ranges in Tables 6a, b and c. Within the tables, the evaluative norms for each communication skill are contained in column a. Thus comparisons can be easily made between the norm (column a), the initial assessment (column b), reassessment (column c) and improvement (column d).

For statistical and presentation reasons the six items for each area of communication skills have been converted to percentages. Six items scored correctly in, for example, the area of money, is recorded as one hundred per cent.

It is obvious that it would be impossible to give equal weighting in difficulty to the thirty items included in the communication sections of the P.A.C.2. Some skill items take far less time to acquire than others. For example, to reach a reading age of nine years from a base line of less than seven years is a much more demanding item than the ability to add coins up to ten pence.

The 't' test is included as a means of assessing whether improvement is significant in areas where P.E.I. norms are not met. It has only been used to assess the significance of the mean improvement of the results for the ten years 1975 and 1977/85 inclusive. Such a measure is particularly required for reading and writing, as significant progress may have been made during the time on classes but not sufficient to meet P.E.I. norms. The reasons why it is difficult to reach P.E.I. norms in reading and writing are discussed below.

Discussion of Results – Basic Education I and II
General (Tables 5, 6a, b and c)

1. The mean number of mild handicapped students for the ten years of assessment is more than the combined numbers for moderate and borderline handicap. The number of moderate handicap has remained low throughout the period.
2. The mean age for the three divisions of handicap is almost identical at thirty, thirty-one years.
3. Mean time on the course is twenty months for all students, except moderate handicap with twenty-four months.
4. In only eighteen out of the one hundred and fifty items shown in the tables for the three divisions of handicap are there instances where the initial assessment meets the P.E.I. norms. This indicates that at initial assessment there was gross under-development in essential communication skills.
5. Improvement was achieved in all items except one for each individual year. The mean improvement for the ten years for the five areas, language, money, time, writing and reading, was significant at the one per cent level using the 't' statistic.

Moderate Handicap (Table 6a)
Language
In six out of the ten years P.E.I. norms were met at initial assessment. At retest P.E.I. norms were attained in each year. Overall for the ten years a retest mean of 49 was well above the P.E.I. norm.

Money
Initial assessment shows gross underfunction. Improvement was made in all years, meeting P.E.I. norms in six of them. Overall for the ten years the P.E.I. norm was attained.

Time
Initial assessment indicates poor time skills. In seven years P.E.I. norms were reached at reassessment with improvement occurring in the remaining three years. A considerable mean improvement over the ten years was achieved.

Writing

The mean at initial assessment indicates that the average student could not sign his name. At reassessment this had been acquired, and also the ability to almost reproduce his address accurately. In only three years were P.E.I. norms met, although the mean improvement over the ten years was significant.

Reading

Although improvement was significant, results are disappointing. In only three years were P.E.I. norms reached. The mean retest figure for ten years failed to meet P.E.I. norms by only two percentage points.

Mild Handicap (Table 6b)

Language

P.E.I. norms were reached for each year. There was a significant improvement in performance over the ten years.

Money

High percentage improvements were made for each year except 1985, where the relatively high initial assessment figure made a large improvement less likely. The retest mean for the ten years indicates that the average student attained two items of skill over and above that required to meet P.E.I. levels.

Time

As with money, time skills improved in excess of P.E.I. norms for each of the ten years. A retest mean of 52 for the ten years shows that progress far out-distanced P.E.I. norms.

Writing

At initial assessment the mean initial assessment for ten years was slightly less than half of the P.E.I. norm. Reassessment mean shows that the P.E.I. norm was almost reached, failing by only one per cent unit. However for individual years P.E.I. norms were met on eight occasions.

Reading

There was significant progress in all years, but P.E.I. norms were attained only in the last two years. As with writing, the mean improvement for the ten years failed to meet P.E.I. norm by only one percentage point.

Borderline Handicap (Table 6c)

Language

P.E.I. norms were reached in each year except one. The mean reassessment figure for the ten years indicates that overall P.E.I. norms were met.

Money

A mean of eighty-nine per cent for the ten years indicates that the average student at reassessment was capable of handling amounts of money, including the giving of change, up to five pounds. P.E.I. norms were comfortably attained throughout the period of assessment.

Time

Overall, a satisfactory result, with the mean at reassessment for the ten years meeting P.E.I. norms. In only 1975 and 1978 was there a failure to reach P.E.I. standards.

Writing

A significant mean improvement of twenty-eight per cent for the ten years was achieved. Despite this achievement, improvement was not sufficient to meet P.E.I. norms in individual years, nor for the ten years as a whole.

Reading

Though improvement was significant over the ten years, it failed to meet P.E.I. standard by some margin. This deficit arises out of the inability of the average student to reach a standard where he is reading material aimed at a reading level of nine years. At initial assessment the mean reading age using the Burt Word Reading Test for the years 1980/85 inclusive was 7 years 4 months for borderline students. During the time a student of this ability attended school an average of twenty months, he would have to develop his reading skill at the rate of one month's increase in reading age for each month of attendance to achieve a reading standard of nine years. This is the rate, all things being equal, at which the average child learns to read. There are valid reasons why the average student has not reached a reading age of nine years, a standard which would meet the norm of the third of the six P.A.C.2 reading items. First, he is below average and cannot be expected to learn at the rate of the average person. Therefore in twenty months' attendance he is unlikely to improve his reading by twenty months. Secondly, he is thirty years of age, and having had a lengthy break from education needs a period of adjustment to learning which can take up to six months before progress is seen to be made. Third, he will opt for work at which he is successful. Observation has shown that most students are men, and they prefer work involving number. Fourth, previous experience of education has left them wary of new contact; this, with a low motivation for improvement, presents problems for teaching and learning. Fifth, students as patients are in a special hospital because of severe personality disorders. Certain of these personality problems are particularly inhibiting to learning.

These reasons also in the main apply to areas other than reading and writing. Teaching staff are convinced, however, that reading and writing are intrinsically affected by the factors forming the basis of these reasons, to a greater extent than other skills. Reading and writing are more complex, requiring greater commitment and concentration from students.

Conclusion

Results taken over ten years of the basic education I and II courses show that significant improvement was made in language, money, time, writing and reading by students classified as mentally handicapped. The largest group, that of mild mentally handicapped, additionally almost completely met P.E.I. norms for the five areas of communication skill for the ten year period, failing by only one percentage unit in reading and writing.

Basic Education I and II – Continuous Assessment

The development of checklists related to P.A.C.2 communication skills items has been described above (Chapter IV). As well as providing the teachers with a hierarchy of sub-skills which will assist her in teaching her students to acquire the higher level skill defined in the P.A.C., checklists give opportunity for immediate feed back to the student. This is an important factor in providing motivation both for students and teacher.

Previous to the introduction of checklists there had been no kind of formal continuous assessment. Students had had to rely on assurance from their teacher that progress was satisfactory, and on the results of their annual reassessment on P.A.C.

While students will usually place faith in their teachers' reassurance, they do appear to need an independent measure of their progress.

Unfortunately results from P.A.C. do not always reflect progress made over the year, disappointing both student and teacher. For example it has been stated above that the P.A.C. item, counting coins to ten pence is relatively easier to acquire than a reading standard of nine years if one is illiterate. Nevertheless for a student who starts classes unable to count and recognise coins and appreciate the concept of value, e.g. one coin may represent a value of two or five etc, counting coins to ten pence assumes the learning of a number of sub-skills if it is ever to be acquired successfully. With a system of continuous reassessment sub-skill acquisition is given recognition as it occurs. At reassessment on P.A.C. a failure on counting coins to ten pence can be assessed in relationship to the progress made on the related check-list.

The system of continuous assessment introduced into the basic education I and II programme is perhaps a more sensitive instrument of progress than P.A.C. It is more capable of providing students with relevant information on progress, thus both giving reassurance and maintaining motivation. Additionally the information it provides is important in recording a more accurate representation of progress in reports to responsible medical officers and other disciplines.

The continuous assessment process of basic education I and II based on checklists has not, as yet, been used in the manner of the P.A.C.2 system to evaluate the effectiveness of the education programme.

The Development of Social Competence
(b) *Basic Education Level III (Basic Studies)*

The evaluation of the basic studies course is presented in two parts: 1. An evaluation based on a continuous assessment process which has been described elsewhere (Bennett, B., 1980). 2. A formal evaluation based on results obtained from Basic Studies Assessment Tests (B.S.A.T.) and standardised reading and spelling tests for the four academic years 1982/83 to 1985/86 inclusive.

1. *Evaluation of the Basic Studies Course Using Results from the System of Continuous Assessment*

A full description of this evaluation was published in March 1980 (Bennett, B., 1980: 378-385). The following extracts are reproduced by kind permission of the editors of *Adult and Continuing Education.*

Objectives of the Evaluation

1. To determine the average attainments of students who had been on the course from twelve to twenty-four months. 2. To examine when

assessments were recorded by reference to the periods (a) first three months, (b) fourth to twelfth months, and (c) thirteen to twenty-four months. 3. To assess the validity of using the average attainment of all students in all skills as an evaluation index, i.e. the minimum level of competence one would accept as satisfactory for students on the course. 4. To assess how far the advantages we had anticipated have been realised by using a structured approach. 5. To review the need to make changes to our approach.

Method

The evaluation of our basic studies structure consisted of three stages. Firstly, results of attainment recorded for students on the course were collected and analysed. Secondly, the objective data obtained from this analysis, and experience of using the structure over two years were discussed by staff. Finally, decisions regarding revision and amendments of the basic studies course were taken.

The instruments used to obtain objective data of students' attainment were our Basic Studies Assessments Charts: Chart I – First Category Attainments, i.e. basic skills, and Chart II – Second Category Attainments, i.e. functional skills.

Table 7a. Sum Totals and Mean Percentages of Attainments achieved on Basic Studies Assessment, Chart 1 – First Category Attainments at 0 to 3, 4 to 11, 13 to 24 months.

	N = 26 (22m 4f)									
	Sum Totals (No) and Mean Percentages of Attainments (%)									
	0 to 3m		*4 to 11m*		*13 to 24m*		*Not dated*		*Totals*	
Area of Skill	*No.*	*%*	*No.*	*%*	*No.*	*%*	*No.*	*%*	*No.*	*%*
Writing										
Legibility	34	26½	27	20½	10	8	4	3	75	58
Spelling	4	3	25	19	4	3	4	3	37	28
Construction	14	11	18	14	26	20	0	0	58	45
Totals	52	13	70	18	40	10	8	2	170	43
Reading										
Accuracy	87	67	8	6	0	0	0	0	95	73
Comprehension	39	30	17	13	1	1	0	0	57	44
Arithmetic										
Mental	23½	18	28	22	16	12	9	7	76½	59
Basic Processes	29	22½	34	26½	12	9½	2	1½	77	60
Parts of Wholes	6	4½	9	7	11	8½	0	0	26	20
Measurement	3	2½	28	21½	23	17½	1	½	55	42
Totals	61½	12	99	19	62	12	12	2	234½	45
Totals – all skills	239½	20	194	17	103	9	20	2	556½	48
Total Attainments Possible All Skills									1,170	100

Table 7b. Sum Totals and Mean Percentages of Attainments achieved on Basic Studies Assessment, Chart II – Second Category Attainments at 0 to 3, 4 to 11, 13 to 24 months.

	N = 26 (22m 4f)									
	Sum Totals (No) and Mean Percentages of Attainments (%)									
	0 to 3m		*4 to 11m*		*13 to 24m*		*Not dated*		*Totals*	
Area of Skill	*No.*	*%*	*No.*	*%*	*No.*	*%*	*No.*	*%*	*No.*	*%*
Letter Writing	6	5½	20	19¼	26	25¼	7	6½	59	57
Wages	10	9½	14	13¾	40	38	–	–	64	61½
Budgeting I	1	¾	8	7¾	26	25	2	1¾	37	35
Budgeting II	3	2¾	8	7¾	21	20¼	1	¾	33	31½
Social Knowledge I	5	4¾	18	17½	13	12¾	1	¾	37	35
Social Knowledge II	10	9½	28	27¼	17	16½	4	3¾	59	57½
Form Filling	14	13¾	17	16½	19	18½	5	4¾	55	52½
Travel/Transport	4	3¾	8	7¾	13	12¾	4	3¾	29	28
Personal Knowledge and Health	25	24	18	17½	36	34½	3	2¾	82	79
Totals – all skills	78	8	139	15	211	22½	27	3	455	48½
Total Attainments Possible All Skills									936	100

Tables 7a and 7b show the areas of skill these charts are designed to assess. Two standardised reading tests, (a) Burt Rearranged Word Reading Test (1967) – accuracy, (b) G.A.P. Reading Comprehension Tests (McLeod, J., 1970) were the only standardised tests used in assessing attainment. Other than reading accuracy and comprehension, none of the items in each area of skill was formally assessed prior to the student starting the course. Assessment was continuous, i.e. attainments were recorded at any time as long as the relevant criteria were met.

The information collected from students' record charts for the evaluation is fundamentally a record of attainment. Without initial assessments with which to compare this information it is very difficult to assess objectively the mean degree of progress made by students. Later in the Discussion section it is suggested, somewhat tentatively, that recordings made in the second year of the course could be indications of progress.

The assessment charts of forty students were examined. Information from each chart was collated for the following categories: (a) sex, (b) ability range, (c) length on course, (d) attainments for each item of each area of skill in both charts at (i) one to three, (ii) four to twelve, (iii) thirteen to twenty-four months. The students had attended classes for from three to four hours weekly for forty weeks a year.

Sixteen students had been on the course for less than twelve months, and their results were not used for the evaluation. The remaining twenty-six students (twenty-two male and four female) had attended for a minimum of one and a maximum of two academic years.

The Ability Range placement of students was as follows: (a) Mild Handicap (I.Q. 55 to 69) – two students, (b) Borderline Handicap (I.Q. 70 to 84) – sixteen students, (c) Dull Average (I.Q. 85-99) – six students, and (d) Bright Average (I.Q. 100 to 114) – one student; one student was unclassified.

The attainments recorded for each assessment item for each area of skill were summed for the total twenty-six students, and the mean percentage attainments for each student calculated.

In Chart I skills there are five assessment items for each area of skill, and in Chart II four. The resultant means, being therefore in the range 1 to 5 or 1 to 4, would, we decided, be better expressed as percentages of the maximum attainment possible for each area of skill or skills. This is shown in the Tables 7a and 7b.

In order to establish at what points on the course attainments were recorded, mean percentage attainments for the periods (a) one to three months, (b) four to eleven, and (c) twelve to twenty-four months were calculated.

Results of Analysis of Attainment

A summary of the results obtained is shown in Tables 7a and 7b. The mean attainments in all skills for both Chart I and II were almost identical, i.e. 48% and 48.5%. Most recordings were made in the first twelve months for both charts. This was more marked for Chart I. In Chart II the percentage recorded in the first twelve months was only slightly higher than in the second twelve months. The lowest recording for writing skills in Chart I was spelling. Construction (Writing) was one of the four Chart I skills where the rate of recording was maintained in the third period. The mean reading accuracy score expressed as reading age was 11 years 11 months, only one month less than the standard (12 years) below which an adult is adjudged to be backward in reading. The mean for Reading Comprehension lagged behind accuracy, at 10 years 8 months.

In the area of arithmetic, results indicated that skill in addition and subtraction were generally satisfactory. Multiplication and division skills were relatively poorly developed. The weakness in these two skills might partially account for the poor development in Parts of Wholes, which had the lowest result in Chart I skills. Measurement showed a good rate of recording in the second twelve months.

In Chart II skills highest recordings were for Personal Knowledge and Health, and Wages. Disappointing results were recorded for the essential skills of Budgeting.

It was assumed that students who ranked high on Chart I skills would also rank high on Chart II. A Spearman Rank-order coefficient of correlation between the results obtained for the two charts was carried out. The result was a positive correlation p 0.6. Perhaps one would have expected a higher correlation. However, there were significant differences between the rankings of several students on both charts which must have depressed the correlation. In particular, one student was only ranked seventeenth on Chart I (i.e. fundamental basic skills) but was second on Chart II (applied skills).

One other interesting point was that this student only ranked twenty-fourth for reading comprehension (R.A. 8y 5m). The student who was placed first in Chart II fared little better, ranking twentieth (R.A. 8y 11m) in reading comprehension. Both students had reached the top two places on Chart II skills with a level of reading comprehension ability, as measured by a standardised test, one would normally consider to be totally inadequate.

Discussion

For lack of space our discussion of results and our experiences must be brief. The following section listing decisions reached as a result of our evaluation may give some indication as to the full range of our discussions. In discussing the results, our first reaction was one of surprise to find that the majority of students fell into the categories of mild and borderline mentally handicapped. Normally, I feel we should have been disappointed in an attainment rate of forty-eight per cent for all skills over a period of twelve to twenty-four months. However, as we knew that eighteen of the twenty-six students were below average ability, the rate appeared to us reasonably satisfactory. It was not unexpected that the majority of recordings were made in the first twelve months, i.e. periods 0 to 3 and 4 to 11 months. As we did not have an initial assessment, it is evident that during this period we were recording attainments acquired before attendance at classes, plus relearning of previously held knowledge and skills in addition to new material. The effects of the course in increasing students' learning can only be fairly judged by reference to attainments recorded in the second twelve months' period. While a nine per cent recording for Chart I attainments is disappointing, a figure of twenty-two and a half per cent for Chart II is encouraging.

What impressed us most, in the reading results, was not the relatively high average ability of the group, as measured by standardised reading tests, but the fact that two students, as mentioned above, were the most successful in Chart II skills, with comprehension reading ages of less than nine. Their teacher attributes their success to two factors: (a) motivation, and (b) maturity. Both study in their own time and show an appreciation of the problems which they will face on discharge. That they were most successful in the functional skills, i.e. Chart II, with relatively limited basic skills, i.e. Chart I, should be a constant reminder that will-power can very often compensate for lack of resources. It is also a warning not to take results obtained from standardised reading tests as indicators of all-round potential.

In considering how far the advantages of the structure had been achieved after two years of use, staff felt that in general we were fulfilling our goals. Reservations have already been expressed about our ability to monitor progress objectively without a basic assessment as a base line. We trust that by the next evaluation these will have been resolved. Additionally, we do not feel the evaluation has provided sufficient information for us to produce with confidence acceptable levels of attainment related to students' potential. We had hoped that these levels would act as guides when decisions had to be made about taking students off the course. If the two students who had barely the minimum standards for acceptance on the course could do so well on Chart II skills, i.e. the more important skills because they are functional, then perhaps we should set as our goal the completion of Chart II as our basic requirement for judging whether a student has completed the course satisfactorily.

2. *Formal Evaluation Basic Education, Level III (Basic Studies) 1982-86*

Following the evaluation of basic studies using continuous assessment results, it was decided that a teacher's knowledge of a student when he was placed on classes was inadequate. Staff considered that a procedure was required for basic studies similar to the P.A.C. Such a procedure would identify needs within the parameters of the basic studies course. It could be used diagnostically, identifying both strengths and weaknesses, knowledge which would enhance a teacher's planning and preparation in the early weeks of a student's placement. Additionally the procedure could be used to evaluate the basic studies course providing opportunity for the establishment of base lines against which subsequent testing could be measured.

In the formulation of a satisfactory procedure it was evident that all areas covered by the basic studies course should be sampled.

The reading tests included in the continuous assessment, viz Burt Rearranged Word Reading Test (1967) and G.A.P. Reading Comprehension Tests (McLeod, J., 1970) would form the reading part of the procedure.

Formal assessment of spelling would be carried out using the Aycliffe Revised Spelling Word List (1973).

Other than these three commercial tests, no further tests were available which would meet the department's needs. Consequently tests had to be developed which were specific to the structure of the basic studies course. These tests are known as the Basic Studies Assessment Tests (B.S.A.T.).

In assessing the writing skills set out in both Charts I and Charts II of the continuous assessment procedure (Table 7a and 7b) it was decided that a single piece of written work, in this case a letter to a friend, would provide information on a student's ability. The letter was to be assessed according to a number of criteria based on legibility, functional spelling, construction, interest, descriptive ability and the conventional presentation of a letter. An item analysis of sixteen criteria was carried out: fourteen were acceptable and now form the basis of the assessment. Test-Retest reliability studies were carried out on fifty students by two raters: results initial test $R1 = 0.71$ and retest, $R2 = 0.65$. Inter-raters reliability on initial test was $R = 0.89$ and on post test $R = 0.91$. These correlations of reliability are acceptable in using the B.S.A.T. 'Write a Letter', as an instrument measuring writing skill.

It was important in developing tests that the number should be as small as possible without any reduction in efficiency, otherwise the battery could be unwieldly and cumbersome. Consideration was given to the design of a test of social knowledge covering most items in Chart II (Table 7b) of the continuous assessment. It was decided that the test should be multiple choice, covering employment, wages, 'best buys', banking, government (local and central), trade unions, health, travel and transport and classification.

111

Originally the prototype test had fifty-nine items. After item analysis twenty items were retained and form the structure of the existing B.S.A.T. Social Knowledge.

The test of reliability carried out using a test-retest procedure gave a correlation of R = 0.82.

The design of a test for number caused some concern, as both Charts I and II (Tables 7a and 7b) contain large areas of skill under this category. It was decided there should be five tests, under mental arithmetic, written addition, subtraction, multiplication and division. Each of the tests would have ten items with each item testing a different concept, skill or knowledge.

Item analysis eventually produced ten items for each of the five test areas.

In tests of reliability the fifty items from the five areas of number were considered together. A correlation of R = 0.82 was achieved on test-retest reliability and R = 0.92 on a split-test reliability on the initial assessment.

The basic studies battery of tests for formal assessment therefore consists of the Burt Word Rearranged Reading Test, the G.A.P. Reading Comprehension Test, the Aycliffe Revised Spelling Word List and B.S.A.T. 'Write a Letter', Social Knowledge, Addition, Subtraction, Multiplication, Division and Mental Arithmetic.

Tables 8a, b, c and d contain results on test and retest on the basic studies test battery for the four academic years 1982/86.

Unlike the P.A.C./P.E.I. procedure there is no external standard against which the results of the basic studies course over the four years can be evaluated. The mean average improvement shown for each year is obtained in the same way as for the P.A.C.2 assessment. That is, progress is measured by comparison of mean performance at initial testing with that obtained in the year of retest. The significance of this progress is evaluated using the 't' statistic. Evaluation of progress on basic studies is therefore considered in relation to the significance of changes between test and retest.

Discussion of Results – Basic Studies Formal Assessment
General (Tables 8a, b, c, d)

1. The number of students reassessed varied between a minimum of 18 in 1983/84 to a maximum of 33 in 1984/85. These numbers are far lower than those for places available on the course. Reasons for this discrepancy are similar to those given above for a similar situation in respect of basic education I and II.

2. The average age is slightly above that given for basic education I and II, but on the whole so similar as to indicate that the average student on one of the basic education courses is in his early thirties.

Tables 8a to 8d. Details of Assessment, Reassessment and Improvement – Basic Studies Course 1982-86

Table 8a.

Academic Year	No. of Students	Mean Age	Mean Time on Course (months)
1982/83	20	32	12
83/84	18	34	16
84/85	33	33	20
85/86	22	31	22
Mean for the four years 1982/86	23	33	18

Table 8b.

	Reading Accuracy				Reading Comprehension			
Academic Years	a	b	c	d	a	b	c	d
1982/83	11yr 6m	11yr 10m	4m	3	10yr 3m	10yr 9m	†6m	2
83/84	11yr 9m	12yr 6m	†9m	2	10yr 5m	11yr 6m	†13m	3
84/85	10yr 9m	11yr 4m	†7m	4	9yr	10yr 3m	†15m	8
85/86	10yr 8m	11yr 5m	†9m	1	10yr 1m	10yr 8m	†7m	4

	Writing				Spelling			
Academic Years	a	b	c	d	a	b	c	d
1982/83	57	71	†14	4	10yr	10yr 3m	*3m	3
83/84	63	73	*10	2	11yr 4m	11yr 8m	*4m	2
84/85	55	69	†14	3	9yr 2m	9yr 5m	*3m	4
85/86	50	65	†15	2	9yr 8m	10yr 2m	*4m	6

Table 8c.

	Social Knowledge				Mental Arithmetic			
Academic Years	a	b	c	d	a	b	c	d
1982/83	58	62	4	7	67	77	10	6
83/84	54	64	*10	5	60	79	†19	4
84/85	49	52	3	11	59	62	3	7
85/86	53	59	6	5	58	71	*13	2

Table 8d.

Academic Years	Addition				Subtraction			
	a	b	c	d	a	b	c	d
1982/83	53	71	†18	1	51	64	*13	3
83/84	56	76	†20	1	42	53	*11	3
84/85	59	69	†10	4	33	46	†13	2
85/86	49	67	†18	2	41	62	†21	1

Academic Years	Multiplication				Division			
	a	b	c	d	a	b	c	d
1982/83	30	42	†12	4	19	36	†17	2
83/84	24	45	†21	3	23	34	*11	3
84/85	26	45	†19	4	22	36	†14	5
85/86	34	48	†14	3	23	39	†16	2

Notes Tables 8b, c and d
Column   a   Mean at initial assessment
Column   b   Mean at reassessment
Column   c   Mean improvement
Column   d   Number of students scoring lower at reassessment than at assessment
†   Indicates Significant at 1% level
*   Indicates Significant at 5% level

3. The mean time on the course is less than for levels I and II, being eighteen as opposed to twenty to twenty-four months. Time spent on basic studies therefore is relatively short considering that in addition to the eighteen months' attendance the full weekly attendance for four hours is rarely achieved due to factors considered above (Chapter II).

    Availability of time for study should be taken into account in considering the evaluation of the results presented in Tables 8a, b, c, d.

4. Tables of results show, in addition to initial test (column a), retest (column b), and progress (column c) an additional column to those recorded for the basic education I and II, P.A.C.2, evaluation. This is column 'd' which shows the numbers of students who recorded a lower score on retesting than on initial assessment. A greater fluctuation of behaviour is likely to occur in students still manifesting signs of mental illness or severe personality disorder than in the normal population. It is likely because of this that some students will, at the time of retest, score lower than they did previously.

5. A positive difference is recorded for all items in every year between test and retest results.

Discussion of Results – Specific Areas of Skill
Reading Accuracy (Table 8b)

The majority of students on basic studies receive no formal instruction in reading. It is assumed that contact with reading material on the course, coupled with teacher intervention and assistance when this is required, will produce reading development. In three out of the four years' assessments on the Burt R.W.R.T. progress was significant at the one per cent level.

Reading Comprehension (Table 8b)

Results indicate that students both at initial test and reassessment do not understand at as high a level as they read accurately. There is therefore an element of 'barking at print'. Nevertheless progress in comprehension was better than that for accuracy in three out of the four years and was significant at the one per cent level in all years.

Although no formal check of records has been carried out to substantiate the belief, it is observed that a significant number of mentally ill patients have a much lower level of comprehension than accuracy development in reading at initial assessment. Usually they will make good progress on classes in comprehension, seeming to reacquire skill rather than developing new competence. It would appear their mental illness, while affecting their comprehension, does not reduce reading accuracy skill.

The biggest mean improvement was in 1984/85 with a figure of fifteen months. This was achieved despite the fact that a quarter of the students scored lower than at initial assessment. However this regression was marginal, whereas five students showing considerable remission from their psychiatric symptoms made twenty to forty months' progress.

Writing (Table 8b)

Progress was made in all four years. This was significant at the one per cent level in three years.

Spelling (Table 8b)

Formal spelling ability as assessed by the Aycliffe Test showed smaller gains than in reading. Though progress was significant this was at either two or five per cent levels.

Social Knowledge (Table 8c)

Results in this area are disappointing. Progress was made in all years, but this was only significant (two per cent level) in 1983/84. There are two possible explanations for the situation. First, staff are aware that most emphasis has been placed on those skills listed under Chart I (Table 7a). Chart II skills (Table 7b) have been relatively neglected, and as these are the areas covered by the Social Knowledge B.S.A.T. test, the lack of progress can be explained by the failure to give them sufficient attention. In an attempt to overcome this problem the course structure is to be changed. A quarter of the weekly basic studies time will be formally allocated to Chart II (Social Skills). The areas of skill or subjects will be presented as modules of learning to groups of students. Each module will last for six to eight weeks. Teaching staff will specialise in one or two subjects. Students will therefore be with their own teacher for three quarters of the weekly allocation of time, working on their personal individualised programmes, and spend the remaining time in an organised group receiving tuition in a subject area of social knowledge.

A second explanation is that the skills listed in Chart II (Table 7b) are now so far removed from the student's reality that they have no immediate meaning. His lack of contact with them through his enforced stay in a closed institution results in an inability to do any more than cling on to those which he has already acquired.

Progress in the area of social knowledge may be small as reported by these results. Nevertheless for the overall sample there has been no general regression and therefore no tendency towards a state of institutionalisation. In a sense the worst effects of a lengthy stay in a closed institution have not caught up with the student. The positive position, therefore, is that in general students have maintained their attainments in a situation where it might be accepted they would normally lose them. However, this statement must be considered in relation to the numbers of students in each of the four years who scored less on reassessment. In 1984/85 this was a third of the total sample.

On balance teaching staff are optimistic that significant progress can be made in social knowledge under the new structure. They accept that insufficient progress may have been made because of an over-emphasis on other areas, with relative inattention to social knowledge.

Mental Arithmetic (Table 8c)

There are wide discrepancies in progress in this area over the four years. In 1983/84 progress was significant at one per cent, while in the following year it was minimal, returning to significance at two per cent in 1985/86. As with reading comprehension, this is an area in which attainment would appear to be more susceptible than other areas to changes in the mental state of students. Three students in 1984/85 on reassessment showed levels of regression of forty per cent.

Addition (Table 8d)

Highly significant progress was made in all four years. The final average level of attainment of approximately seventy per cent would seem to be an acceptable level of competence.

Subtraction (Table 8d)

Progress was satisfactory at either the two or one per cent levels. Nevertheless final average attainments indicate that further learning opportunities are required.

Multiplication (Table 8d)

Base line assessments show poor development at initial assessment. Significant progress at the one per cent level was made. An average attainment of between forty and fifty per cent at reassessment points to the necessity for further educational intervention.

Division (Table 8d)

Initial assessments were even lower than for multiplication. Progress was significant but not sufficient to state that final overall competence was satisfactory.

Further Comment

Results from the arithmetic tests show that students have made significant progress. Nevertheless there is a realisation that the majority need to enhance their ability to calculate not only through traditional 'summing' methods but through the use of calculators. Students are now taught the advantages of calculators and how to use them.

Conclusion — Evaluation Basic Studies

Students, over a four year period of assessment, made progress in all areas of the basic studies course. This progress was significant in most areas throughout the four years. Social knowledge was an area in which progress was not significant. It was accepted that sufficient time in the basic studies course had not been allocated to this area. Steps are being taken to ensure that this situation is rectified.

The Development of Social Competence
Basic Education Evaluation
Case Studies

Kevin

At initial assessment Kevin's I.Q. was 49 (moderate handicap). He did not know the names of letters or their sounds and was unable to read any social signs e.g. LADIES, TOILETS etc. Writing skill was non-existent. He had great difficulty in copying standard shapes, e.g. square, triangle etc. Visual and auditory discrimination were very poor and he had problems with spatial position and direction. He was clumsy, had poor balance, difficulty in catching and throwing, and slowness in responding to cues. Overall cognitive development was equivalent to a child of three years. Educational prognosis was stated (independently) to be poor.

Kevin attended level I (morning for three years), progressing to level II (three afternoons weekly) for a further year. Assessed by an external psychologist at the time of his transfer to a local authority hostel, his I.Q. was now 60. The psychologist wrote:

"Kevin demonstrated his newly acquired skills. He wrote his name and address legibly without error and was able to name coins and show understanding of their relative values. Although he would have scored poorly on a standard reading test, Kevin was able to read approximately three hundred social signs, tell the time, handle money, measure and complete simple forms unaided."

Sharon

Sharon had to be interviewed using her 'Teddy Bear' as an intermediary. Her behaviour was at an infantile level and even P.A.C.2 items were too advanced for her. Initially on school she would only communicate through 'Teddy'. She preferred to sit on the floor, rocking to and fro with frequent incidences of incontinence.

Currently preparing for discharge, Sharon has reacquired many skills and is working competently at a level befitting an average school-leaver. Her improvement has been facilitated by the skilled care she has received by all disciplines in the hospital.

Ronald

Ronald had been in Rampton Hospital for many years. He had been recommended for basic education but had always refused. His psychiatrist was concerned at Ronald's poor level of social competence at a time when Ronald was being considered for discharge. Reluctantly Ronald, after considerable persuasion from his doctor and charge nurse and reassurance from teaching staff, decided to attend classes. Over a period of six months he would try every conceivable dodge not to attend classes and frequently requested to be taken off education. There was then a significant change, which in the light of his previous behaviour was difficult to explain. Ronald began to attend regularly, work harder, and be more pleasant. It did not seem appropriate to ask Ronald at the time about this change of heart, but some time later when he had been transferred to the Eastdale Unit at Balderton Hospital, Newark, he was asked what prompted him to study hard. He said that he had started to think about himself in relation to the services offered by the education department in the time before he went to sleep each night. From his deliberation he began to admit to himself there were many areas in which his skills and knowledge were inadequate. Additionally he recognised that these limitations caused him to feel uncomfortable, self-conscious and on occasions helpless in situations where other people appeared to cope with ease. For example, he mentioned his love of darts and how this was frustrated by an inability to score with a reasonable facility. He was also very conscious of his failure in writing letters and admitted to feeling uncomfortable in a shop because of his lack of social skills.

There had therefore been a noticeable development of Ronald's perception of himself and awareness of the need to change. The education department provided the opportunity for change not only in basic education and related life and social skills but in other areas too. As Ronald said, although he had now learned to swim while on classes this had been achieved concurrently with a feeling of regret that he had waited so long to enjoy the activity.

Through his involvement in basic education and swimming Ronald would seem to have made great strides in his personal development. His former lethargy and indifference were replaced by a willingness to try and improve himself. The most heartening aspect of this change of heart was that the motivation has stemmed from his own perceptions of his inadequacies.

Personal Development — Evaluation

Though it was not found possible to evaluate development in social competence as a whole, it was possible to quantify progression in certain areas of this concept. The evaluation of personal development does not offer us even this restricted opportunity except perhaps in one area: the exception being the opportunity in the education department to further one's development through academic or vocational study. Although perhaps a poor measure with which to measure personal development, Table 9 shows the results of the relatively few students who have been assessed through external examinations. Their results are an indication of their success in coping with the demands of study and the skill of presentation of what they know.

Other evidence that personal development is enhanced is mainly anecdotal. There are examples of psychiatrists expressing opinions about the value of the education experience to an individual's development. Equally students have given their views of the meaning of education in their lives. Teachers also can recall vividly students who in their opinion have made great strides in personal development during their time on school.

Finally, a novel experience like the annual Summer School provides an opportunity to gauge students' reactions to the experiences the event provides.

Evaluation of Personal Development — Academic Success

Table 9 is the complete record of students' academic (and vocational) success as measured by examination passes since the education department opened in 1969. Until the late seventies entries were almost entirely restricted to the General Certificate of Education. Since then a wider range of examinations have become available.

Considering the large number of patients who have been treated at Rampton Hospital since 1969 the number of examination passes is low. Nevertheless until recently it was official policy to admit only patients of low intelligence to the hospital. Until recently those of higher intelligence have been referred to Broadmoor Hospital and more recently to Park Lane Hospital. In general there is a trend for this policy to continue but there is evidence to indicate that Rampton now receives a higher proportion of average and above average patients.

The G.C.E. results show that the education department is able to provide by one means or another resources for study in a wide range of subjects. Opportunity is not restricted by an inability to organise classes in particular subjects.

Evaluation of Personal Development — Anecdotal

In posing the question whether education has assisted patients to find interest, stimulation and a higher appreciation of life, one is aware of the difficulty in giving answers which are completely satisfactory. Although it is possible to give anecdotal accounts related to the success of individual students, this cannot be claimed to demonstrate that overall for all students attending the education department there have been significant strides in personal development.

Teaching staff would be first to reject an assertion that in all cases there is an obvious relationship between attendance at education and personal development. This is based on the experience of teaching a number of patients who, while making progress in cognitive and practical skills, continue to exhibit anti-social attitudes and a lack of insight into their problems.

Other disciplines are perhaps not so reticent in making claims for education. In particular several psychiatrists have expressed the opinion that the main reason they require their patients to attend the education department is to benefit from the social interaction and 'therapeutic atmosphere'; the 'explicit' curriculum being secondary to this objective.

In the provision of basic education there has been some disagreement with psychiatrists over the question of the priority of objectives. During the late 1970s such was the pressure for places on basic education that a procedure was formalised whereby those students who had achieved their objectives or had failed to make significant progress over a long period of time were taken off classes. This was not a final parting with education, for arrangements were made to review such patients at frequent intervals, and, with some, arrange for a weekly tutorial on the ward. One psychiatrist objected very strongly to this arrangement, as it resulted in patients being deprived of the valuable and irreplaceable

Table 9. Record of Examination Passes 1971-86

Name of Examination Board	Examination	Subject	Grade & Level	Total No. of Passes including merit awards	Period
Associated	G.C.E.	Art	O	6	1971-86
Examining Board	G.C.E.	Art History	O	1	1971-86
(A.E.B.)	G.C.E.	Computer Studies	O	2	1971-86
	G.C.E.	Economics	A	1	1971-86
	G.C.E.	English Lang.	O	16	1971-86
	G.C.E.	English Lit.	O	1	1971-86
	G.C.E.	Geometrical Drawing	O	1	1971-86
	G.C.E.	Geography	O	2	1971-86
	G.C.E.	German	O	1	1971-86
	G.C.E.	History	O	2	1971-86
	G.C.E.	Human Biology	O	1	1971-86
	G.C.E.	Maths	O	9	1971-86
	G.C.E.	Russian	O	1	1971-86
			A	1	1971-86
	G.C.E.	Sociology	O	1	1971-86
				46 Total G.C.E. Passes	
A.E.B.	Basic English	English		9 Total Passes	1984-86
East Midland Examining Board	Basic Numeracy	Mathematics		16 Total Passes	1982-86
Royal Society of Arts Examinations Board (R.S.A.)		Arithmetic	Stage I	17	1978-86
		Arithmetic	Stage II	2	
		English	Stage I	9	
				28 Total Passes	
R.S.A.		Typing	S1	5	1978-82
			S2	2	
				7 Total Passes	
East Midland Examinations Union (Now East Midlands Further Education Council)	City & Guilds	Basic Cookery for Catering Industry	S1	21	1977-80
Validation by West Notts College of F.E.		Basic Cookery for Catering Industry		11	1980-85
				32 Total Passes	

social interaction which existed in the department. The education department was seen to be one area in the hospital where it was likely patients would become more self-aware and develop at the same time valuable social skills.

The attitude of the psychiatrist was a compliment to the education department. It showed in all respects perhaps a wider recognition of the value of education in relationship to personal development (or perhaps redevelopment for the mentally ill) than was acknowledged by teaching staff. The opinion of the particular psychiatrist and of a number of colleagues is of some significant value in claiming that education at Rampton generally assists in personal development. There is no, cast iron evidence to support the claim, but psychiatrists are professionals whose opinions are highly valued, consequently their views should be treated with respect.

Although teaching staff would not agree that involvement in education does of necessity enhance personal development, they are aware of dramatic changes occurring in patients during the time they have attended classes. In recognising these changes they are also sensitive to the need to acknowledge that the changes cannot be solely attributable to attendance at the education department.

An illustrative example of this position is the case of Jimmy. Jimmy was short, aggressive, hostile, extremely volatile, over-sensitive and verbally and physically abusive. On the main wards his charge nurse and various staff nurses became aware that beneath this formidable inventory of anti-social attitude and behaviour there was a personality desperately seeking a way out of its current plight. Many hours were spent by these good men in helping Jimmy come to terms with himself.

The physical education programme run by the education department seemed a reasonable facility for providing Jimmy with an outlet in which he could express his physical aggression in a socially acceptable form. In the early days of involvement in such games as soccer, basketball and hockey Jimmy's temper bettered him on numerous occasions. He spent a good deal of time on the sidelines 'cooling down'. Gradually Jimmy learnt to channel his aggression into the activities. He became an excellent soccer player with boundless energy which was difficult to match. In athletics he showed enormous potential as a sprinter, achieving 'evens' for the hundred yards on many occasions.

The success he achieved in the physical education programme was reinforced by the fatherly advice and attention he was receiving from his nurses. There were fewer episodes of pacing up and down fulminating at all and sundry. Smiles and the ability to give and take banter became more frequent.

Jimmy liked himself more and was liked by an increasing number of people. His occupation officers played a major role in Jimmy's rehabilitation, for as he became more aware of what he was capable of, these officers were able to teach him the trade of tailoring; a trade Jimmy was able to follow on his subsequent discharge.

Jimmy's improvement in personal development came about, therefore, because of the skilled intervention of a number of disciplines; each discipline making a major contribution to his rehabilitation.

Perhaps the antithesis of Jimmy is "Just Nicholl". Whereas Jimmy was completely lost and needed considerable assistance to find his way in life, "Just Nicholl" had a clear idea of how he should use his time in the hospital and the reasons for doing so. This is not to suggest that "Just Nicholl" rejected help and assistance: on the contrary he was most anxious to assist in the therapeutic process which leads to discharge. However, "Just Nicholl" could point to a long connection with education from the days when he was a staunch member and supporter of the N.C.L.C. (The National Council for Labour Colleges). He was, and had been convinced for a considerable time of the power of education as a medium of change. This is shown in his writing of an account in the patients' magazine called "Education — Why Bother?". He quoted John Bunyan: "Abandon hope all ye who enter these gates". The gates, as you might have guessed, lead into Rampton Hospital. He then went on:

> "Perhaps the alternative, to me, was to abandon hope and waste my time, day after day, week after week, and let's face it year after year doing the crossword or worse still, watching 'Crossroads'. To me knowledge took on a new and extended meaning. In the words of St. Paul it became 'a new and lively hope', against Bunyan's 'Slough of despair'. It became, to me, no less than the potter's wheel.
>
> No man is a fixed thing, he is forever changing, interacting with and being changed by the people and the forces around him. We may grow more hopeful, more despondent, more cynical, more objective, but change we will because we cannot remain the same. All men are clay on the potter's wheel. Wouldn't (sic) it be better if your own mind shaped the clay, if it was your own hand that was applied to the potter's wheel. What more could anyone want to get from the discipline of education?"
>
> ('Just Nicholl')

Clive was another patient who had an ambition for himself. The education department helped him to achieve this, but Clive had commenced his quest long before he came into contact with education. Clive had, unlike 'Just Nicholl', no educational framework to rely on when he started his ambitious project to learn the Russian language. It would appear he had had little formal education before, as an adolescent, he found himself constrained to life in a hospital for the subnormal.

According to Clive his contact with several Polish patients in Rampton Hospital kindled an ambition to learn Russian. Polish, Clive assured teaching staff, was very similar to Russian. It seemed logical to him to learn the more prestigious of the two languages.

Almost in total isolation Clive started to learn Russian with the help of his Polish friends, text books and tapes. It would be perhaps unkind to say that his approach was obsessive, but there is no doubt that the task to learn the language started on waking and only 'finished' when he was asleep. Each day he planned his strategy. At breakfast each of his fellow patients might be given the name of a verb for the day. Every time each patient was seen Clive would conjugate the verb in the tense which he had selected. Another strategy was practised as he lay in bed. In his mind he would project a classroom in which he was the teacher. Pupils were given tasks to do, sometimes reading, sometimes reciting and at other times writing on the blackboard. These were very sophisticated strategies for someone who had been thought by authority to be in need of care in a hospital for the subnormal.

Initially Clive approached the education department for help in obtaining material for his studies. A 'Linguaphone Course' was purchased, library books were obtained, and a local teacher of Russian provided newspapers and magazines. This teacher also read some of Clive's work and gave his opinion that Clive was certainly 'O' level standard.

Arrangements were made for Clive to take his 'O' level. He passed with the highest grade, 'A1' at that time, but not without a scare in the Russian dictation test. The external examiner and the author were present for the test. At the third attempt Clive was finally convinced that all he had to do was write down in Russian what the examiner dictated to him in Russian. The problem in attempts one and two was that Clive could not accept that an examiner could be asking him to do what was to him a ridiculously easy task. Clive had responded by writing down an English translation of the Russian dictation. This proved to be accurate, but caused a problem to the examiner, for this was not what the examining board required.

Following this success, Clive had earned a right to tutorial support. A teacher of Russian attended the hospital for an hour once a fortnight to prepare Clive for his 'A' level. In his 'A' level examination his oral examiner from the University of East Anglia was greatly impressed by Clive's competence in the language. In particular she rated his accent and spoken fluency as being equal to her best students at the university. It has never ceased to amaze that his oral ability could reach such a high standard while he himself was constrained in the confines of a top security special hospital while learning the language.

Clive attained a 'B' grade in his 'A' level examination. Such a grade would surely be marketable when the time came for Clive to leave the hospital. Clive had, however, other ideas. He stunned those responsible for resettling him in the community with the comment that life in mental hospitals had trained him to be a very good domestic cleaner and this was the type of job he wanted to follow outside. To those who pointed out that his fluent Russian could possibly ensure that he procured a much better paid and higher status of employment, he replied that this was not for sale. The desire to learn Russian had come from within himself. While acknowledging the assistance he had received in recent years, he had nurtured this idea by his own determination. It had given him strength, solace and support with a new meaning to life throughout his stay in the hospital. He trusted that his studies in the language would continue to be his staff in his years ahead outside the hospital.

Clive left Rampton Hospital to work in a Cheshire Home, where his undoubted proficiency as a domestic would be highly valued. There remains a memory, however, of a man who was able to hold back the negative influences of life in a closed institution by his involvement in education. It would be difficult to find a better example of education for personal development in its purest form than Clive's determination to learn the Russian language and subsequently to explore the heritage and culture of Russia through her own tongue.

Space does not allow one the freedom to describe other students who have managed, largely through education, to find personal satisfaction though their lives were confined within the walls of a top-security hospital. David and Norman, for example, enthralled by computers and computing, mastering techniques so successfully they were able to write purpose-designed programmes for severely and profoundly mentally handicapped in a local hospital school. Both working hard for 'O' levels and determined to start an Open University degree next year. Or Raymond, who had great difficulty reading words presented to him

126

individually but could worry at a text until by some form of contextual perception he grasped the gist of its content.

Evaluation of Personal Development — Summer School

The Summer School provides opportunity for personal development both in the acquisition of knowledge and skill and social interaction. The following is the Principal's report for the Summer School 1986. It includes an attempt to evaluate the event through the use of a questionnaire.

SUMMER SCHOOL 1986 — Principal's Report
Introduction:

Following on the success of the 1985 Summer School it was decided not to make any fundamental changes in the programme for 1986. Planning proceeded very much on the lines described in the Report for 1985.

Part 1 — General Description
Dates of Course — 28 July to 1st August inclusive
Subjects offered and tutors:

Soccer Coaching — Jonathan O'Donnell assisted by his friend, Stuart Batchelor (on a voluntary basis) for the last three days.

Music — Ian Newton (assisted by two teaching colleagues on the Wednesday afternoon). These teachers gave a stimulating practical and oral account of the development of guitar music.

Computer Literacy — Kevin Boot.

Art — Peter Searle
The tutors had all been employed the previous year.

Sessions

Morning 9.15 to 10.30, 10.45 to 12.15
Afternoon 1.30 to 2.45, 3.00 to 4.30

Organisation

Students attended the first three sessions for their main subject and took part in an alternative subject for the last session.

Breaks

The morning and afternoon breaks for drinks took place in the areas of activity. Lunch was taken in the Recreation Hall.

Applications to Attend the School

These were made by individual patients on forms prepared by the department.

Number of Applications

Art 26, Computers 23, Soccer 31, Music 16 — Total 96.

Number of Applications Accepted

Soccer 22, Art 11, Music 15, Computers 9.

NOTE At the start of the course, two had to withdraw from soccer because of injury and two from computers because of indisposition.

Final Registrations

Soccer 20, Art 11, Music 15, Computers 7 — Total 53.

Attendance

Monday 46 (86%), Tuesday 45 (85%), Wednesday 49 (92%), Thursday 44 (79%) Friday 39 (70%).

NOTE The Friday attendance was affected by outside trips.

Evaluation

The success of the 1985 Summer School was mainly assessed through the comments of staff and a number of letters received from patients. It was decided for 1986 that each participant should be asked to make comments on the course through the medium of a questionnaire. The intention of this procedure was to prompt a great number of students to comment on various aspects of the course.

Number of Students making returns — 29 (55%).

Responses to Questions
(a) Was your main subject satisfactory?

Yes 28
Fair 1
No 0

(b) Would you choose your main subject again?

Yes 27
Maybe 1
No 1

(c) Was your fourth period option satisfactory?

Yes 24
Fair 1
No Comment 2
No 2

(d) Are there other subjects you would like to see in next year's programme — if so, what are these?

From an organisational point of view the suggestions were not helpful as almost everyone responding made a different suggestion. Eighteen subjects were suggested and the highest support was for swimming which was the choice of three.

Comments made on the Questionnaire
In addition to questions, course members were asked to make general comments on the course.

(a) Length of Course
Fourteen responses requested that the course be longer; the majority of these asked for two weeks.

(b) Personal Satisfaction
Ten students made comments stating how much they had enjoyed the course. One stated that the course should convince hospital staff and patients of the worthwhileness of education!!

(c) Staffing
Four comments were made as follows:
(1) "Staff were excellent".
(2) "I found that the staff during Summer School were very efficient. Contrary to my past attitude I was able to fit more into it this year, thus gaining more from it".
(3) "Activity staff are preferred because they join in the activities".
(4) "Preferable if staff (nursing) in classroom join in".

(d) Catering
(1) "Bread should be available at lunch".
(2) "Tea should be available at lunch".
(3) "Rampton "duff" is regrettably in decline. Lunches would have been more filling if "duff" with custard had been available".
(4) "Sweet not filling enough".

(e) Social
(1) "Music or video should have been provided at lunchtime".
(2) "Grace should be said before taking lunch".
(3) "Mixed soccer should be introduced".

Others
(a) "Sessions should be longer", (b) "The day should be 9.00 to 5.00".

Summary

The response to the questionnaire of fifty per cent was above average for the population for which it was intended (Dave Briggs — Principal Psychologist).

The responses of students as to the success and enjoyment of the course corresponded almost entirely to the views expressed by nursing and teaching staff closely involved in the organisation and administration of the course.

A significant number of students requested a longer course. This request should be explored but initial thoughts on the issue are that a long course would be difficult to implement mainly because of a difficulty in recruiting teaching staff.

Almost everyone was satisfied with the subjects offered and it is difficult to envisage any change for next year if the same lecturers are available. No clear preferences emerged from students' returns for alternative subjects.

Considering the number of alternative commitments the attendance was, as last year, very satisfactory.

Conclusion
The second annual Summer School proved to be a pleasurable, worthwhile and stimulating experience, both for its students and staff.

Evaluation of Personal Development — Conclusion
There is perhaps a feeling that a number of students would resist the despair and dejection of facing life cut off from main-stream society, seeing their predicament as a challenge to be overcome. They would do this irrespective of the type of support that can be provided within special hospitals. Nevertheless the opportunities presented by the education department at Rampton Hospital would appear to have facilitated the ambitions of the committed, while currently motivating less self-stimulated individuals to seek out new skills and knowledge. Experience suggests that education in a closed institution has a marked effect in developing personal growth, thus stultifying the insidious danger of institutional conformity.

Summary
An attempt has been made to evaluate the educational service for patients at Rampton Hospital in three areas, viz (a) the development of an educational service; (b) the development of social competence; (c) the opportunity provided for personal development.

In response to patient needs and institutional pressures there has been significant growth of educational resources in buildings, staffing, materials and equipment since 1969. An analysis of the education department's organisation indicates three major developmental periods. Up to 1975 main emphasis was given to the development of the curriculum for patients with severe handicaps in basic communication skills. In the next five years the major developments were in developing courses in basic literacy, numeracy and social knowledge, and in providing teaching staff for areas of activity outside the main education department. The most recent phase, post Boynton, shows a development towards a department capable of providing a programme of activities as comprehensive as that to be found in a small college of further education.

The evaluation of social competence stressed the difficulty of making categoric statements that social competence was improved by educational intervention. Nevertheless statistics were given both for Basic Education levels I and II courses and for level III (Basic Studies), which showed over a number of years that patients had made significant progress in basic educational skills and knowledge.

The education department sees as a major task the opportunity for patients to make considerable strides in personal development. It was shown by the number of examination successes that some patients have made personal development in the acquisition of knowledge. In areas of personal development which depend on the maturation of a personality that is socially aware and has a realistic appraisal of self, it was acknowledged that relevant and valid evidence was not available. Anecdotal accounts of patients' development were provided which give some indication that the education department does provide a real and apparent stimulus for personal development.

Overall the evidence provided suggests that education in special hospitals has an important part to play in meeting the needs of patients and the attainment of treatment aims.

Chapter VI

FUTURE DEVELOPMENT

Current capital spending on upgrading and improving buildings and other resources would appear to indicate the government's commitment to the retention of special hospitals as a major part of the mental health structure. Special hospitals would seem to have, therefore, a secure future at least well into the next century.

Increased attention to physical treatment in developing resocialisation/rehabilitation policies in special hospitals gives some indication that an educational presence will remain a priority. At Rampton Hospital central resources for education are unlikely to expand much above current levels. Nevertheless the trend to employ teachers to work with colleagues in areas not under the direct control of the senior education officer could continue. There is, for example, current speculation of opening a special area of the occupations department for the day care of a number of patients who are currently reluctant to involve themselves in any activity. It has been suggested by the chief occupation's officer that a teacher should be employed in the area at least part of the day.

Rampton Hospital's continued attempts to improve treatment and care of its patients could have significant effects on the education department. Those problems of patients' attendance discussed in Chapter II could be resolved when the new shift system for nursing is introduced. An overlap of morning and afternoon shifts at lunchtime should ensure a system capable of getting students to the education department for a two o'clock start.

The arrangement whereby the education department was provided with a core staff of six nurses in January 1987 has made significant improvements to the teaching environment in classrooms. Core nursing staff are working regularly with teachers in the classroom. This not only proves efficient in teaching and learning but ensures a safer environment through continuous interactive observation in contrast to the previous practice of a reliance on passive observation.

While the main tasks of the department will continue to be related to the facilitation of social competence and personal development, there will inevitably be a progression through a multidisciplinary approach to involvement in specialised areas such as psychotherapy and counselling.

This will involve only those members of the education department who have shown interest and a facility in these areas and who have been prepared to attend training. Currently registers of accredited therapists, consisting of members of all professions within the hospital who are considered competent in sex education and counselling, and psycho-therapy are being compiled.

It is likely that as the criteria for admission to special hospitals are more strictly applied, the treatment needs of patients will be progres-sively more complex and difficult to meet. There is currently a section of the Rampton Hospital population who face the prospect of very long stays. The education department has a part to play in making the lives of these patients as tolerable and bearable as is possible, through the provision of academic, social, artistic and recreational pursuits.

There are signs that Rampton Hospital is coming to terms with its two most fundamental but diametrically opposed aims — maintenance of a high level of security, and preparation of patients for life in the community. Staffing wards with both male and female staff, a system of internal parole, and an increase in visits as part of the rehabilitation process are examples of the determination of management to make Rampton Hospital a truly therapeutic community. As this development proceeds, the signs are that the work of the education department will continue as in the past to assist the Hospital meet its goals.

BIBLIOGRAPHY

A.P.M.H. (Association of Professions for the Mentally Handicapped). *Statement on the Educational Needs of Mentally Handicapped Adults.*

Aycliffe *Revised Spelling Word List* 1973.

Bender, M. and Valletuti, P. J. *Teaching the Moderately and Severely Handicapped: Curriculum Objectives, Strategies and Objectives. Vol. 1 Behaviour, Self-care and Motor Skill* Baltimore, Union Park Press, 1976.

Bennett, B. 'An Evaluation of the Rampton Basic Studies Course' *Adult Education* Vol.52, No.6, 1980.

Bennett, B. 'A Method for Structuring a Basic Education Course at Rampton Hospital' *Adult Education* Vol. 50, No.1, 1977.

Bennett, B. 'Remedial Education at Rampton' *Special Education Forward Trends* Vol. 3, No.4, 1976.

Boynton, J. (Chairman) *Report of the Review of Rampton Hospital* Commd 8073 H.M.S.O., 1980.

Burt, C. (Revised by Vernon, P. E.) *Burt Rearranged Word Reading Test* Hodder and Stoughton Educational, 1938 to 1976.

Clarke, A. M. and Clarke, A. D. B. (Editors) *Mental Deficiency: The Changing Outlook* 3rd Edition, Methuen, 1974.

Cleckley, H. *The Mask of Sanity* (New American Library) New York, Mosby, 1982.

Clyne, P. *The Disadvantaged Adult* Longman, 1972.

Cohen, S. and Taylor, L. *Psychological Survival* 2nd Edition, Penguin, 1981.

Crissey, M. S. 'Mental Retardation, Past, Present and Future' *American Psychologist* Vol.130, No.8, August 1975.

Elliott, J. R. *A Survey of Rampton Hospital* (Confidential Report) D.H.S.S, 1973.

Forster, W. *Prison Education in England and Wales* Leicester, N.I.A.E., 1987.

Gan, S. and Pullen, G. P. 'The Unicentre: An Activity Centre for the Mentally Ill. The First Two Years' *Occupational Therapy* July 1984.

Goffman, E. *Asylums* Penguin, 1961.

Gunzburg, H. C. *Progress Assessment Chart of Social Development (Form 2)* Stratford-upon Avon, S.E.F.A. (Publication) Ltd., 1974.

Gunzburg, H. C. *Progress Evaluation Index* — 2, Stratford-upon-Avon, S.E.F.A. (Publication) Ltd., 1974.

Gunzburg, H. C. *Social Competence & Mental Handicap* Bailliere, Tindall and Cassell Ltd., 1968.

Hospital Advisory Service *Report on Rampton Hospital* HAS (71(SH)2) 1971.

Itard, J. M. G. (Translated by Humphrey, G. & M.) *The Wild Boy of Aveyron* New York, Meredith Pub. Co., 1962.

Jones, K. *A History of the Mental Health Services* Routledge & Kegan Paul, 1972.

Kellmer Pringle, M. L. *Deprivation and Education* Longman, 1965.

King's Fund Centre Exhibition *How has this happened? The Story of services for the mentally handicapped* (Fact Sheet) London, undated.

Lester — Smith, W. O. *Education* Penguin Books, 1962.

McConville, Sean (Ed) *The Use of Imprisonment* (Essays in the changing state of English penal policy) (Routledge Direct Editing) R. & K.P., 1975.

McLeod, J. and Unwin, D. *G.A.P. Reading Comprehension Test* Heinemann Educational, 1970.

McNally, J. *Key Words Attainment and Diagnostic Test* Schoolmaster Publishing Co., 1968.

McNally, J. and Murray, W. *Key Words to Literacy* (Curriculum Studies No. 3) Schoolmaster Publishing Co., 1968.

Manchester Conference Minutes, June 1974.

Masters, A. *Bedlam* Michael Joseph, 1977.

Mittler, P. (Chairman) *Helping Mentally Handicapped People in Hospital* D.H.S.S., 1978.

Morris, P. *Put Away* R. & K. P., 1969.

Newton, M. J. and Thomson, M. E. *Aston Index* Wisbech, England, L.D.A., Undated.

Newton, M. J. and Thomson, M. E. *Readings in Dyslexia* Wisbech, England, Benrose U.K., 1979.

O'Hara, J. 'The Role of the Nurse in Subnormality' *J. Ment. Sub* Vol. XIV, 1968.

P. P. Reports, Committees, 4, *Estimates 1967/68 Vol.III — Second Report.*

Parker, E. No. 11, *Survey of Incapacity Associated with Mental Handicap at Rampton and Moss Side Special Hospitals* London, Special Hospital Research Unit, 1974.

Pilkington, T. L. *Patterns of Care for the Mentally Retarded in the United Kingdom* Kings Fund Centre Publication 74/306, 1974.

Pilsworth, M. and Ruddock, R. 'Some Criticisms of Survey Research Methods in Adult Education' *Convergences* Vol. VIII, No.2, 1975.

Ross, J. S. *Groundwork of Education Theory* Harrap and Co., 1943.

Scottish Home and Health Department *State Hospital Carstairs* Edinburgh, H.M.S.O., 1977.

Tansley, A. E. *Reading & Remedial Reading* Routledge & Kegan Paul, 1967.

Than, R. *Mental Illness — Its Effect on Educational Attainment & Behaviour: A Pilot Study* (Unpublished Dissertation Advanced Diploma in Special Education) Sheffield, 1982.

Thomson, M. and Norton, M. *Diagnosing Dyslexia in the Classroom: A Preliminary Report* University of Aston, Department of Applied Psychology, Undated.

Wedell, K., 'Diagnosing Learning Difficulties: A Sequential Strategy' *Journal of Learning Difficulties* Vol. 3, No. 6, 1970.

Whelan, E., Speake, B. and Strickland, T. 'The Copewell System' in Dean & Hegarty, S. *Learning for Independence* Further Education Unit, 1984.

Wood Committee. *The Report of the Mental Deficiency Committee Parts I, II, III & IV* H.M.S.O., 1929.

Working Party No.27 *Cross'd with Adversity: the education of socially disadvantaged children in secondary schools* Schools Council for the Curriculum and Examinations, 1970.